Cha

A Mu

— 3 1

Dear Julia,

I hope you enjoy
reading my grandmother's
book, re-published after 75
years. Her analysis and
commentary remains highly
relevant today,

Ari

28/IV/2015

Changing India

A Muslim Woman Speaks

Iqbalunnisa Hussain

OXFORD
UNIVERSITY PRESS

OXFORD
UNIVERSITY PRESS

Oxford University Press is a department of the University of Oxford.
It furthers the University's objective of excellence in research, scholarship,
and education by publishing worldwide. Oxford is a registered trade mark of
Oxford University Press in the UK and in certain other countries

Published in Pakistan by
Ameena Saiyid, Oxford University Press
No. 38, Sector 15, Korangi Industrial Area,
PO Box 8214, Karachi-74900, Pakistan

© Oxford University Press 2015

The moral rights of the author have been asserted

First published in 1940, by Hosali Press, Bangalore, India

This Edition by Oxford University Press, Pakistan, 2015

ISBN 978-0-19-906836-4

Typeset in Minion Pro
Printed on 60gsm Book paper

Printed by VVP

Contents

Foreword

It is said that a prophet is seldom appreciated at home. This was the case with my mother. We failed to realize her sterling character and work. She was a simple village girl. When she was married, her only education was a smattering of Arabic and Urdu. It was my father who gave her learning through correspondence while he was studying in Bombay. It is amazing how she learnt English and was able to produce book after book in fine English.

She bore seven children while acquiring a degree in India and later in the UK. Her thoughts always lay with the unfortunate poor Muslim women: women in pain and trouble who would come to her for help and sympathy. She held them in her arms to comfort them and wept with them. She even went to their husbands, fathers, or brothers, whom she admonished to fight for the women's rights. She showed them the honourable and Muslim way. She threatened them and most often brought peace between them.

This simple, little-educated woman made friends with personalities like Lord and Lady Baden-Powell, Lady Astor [the first female MP], and Pearl Buck [Nobel Laureate in Literature]. She kept correspondence with Princess Durru Shehvar of Hyderabad Deccan and Lady Mirza Ismail [wife of Sir Mirza Ismail], until she passed away. She had a two-hour long interview with Kemal Atatürk.

She also met poet Muhammad Iqbal and painter Abdur Rahman Chughtai, and they both gave her the same book of pictures by Abdul Rahman Chughtai and a book of Omar Khayyam's poetry. She was held in great esteem by all organizations and personalities in India. Yet she was the most unpretentious and humble person possible. I have known her to run and fetch chairs for her children at parties if she found them without a seat.

I am indeed honoured and grateful that I am able to write a few words about her. I could write volumes. We seven children treated her with the utmost honour and respect, which she so richly deserves. I hope this book is a befitting tribute and will make her happy.

All proceeds from this publication will go to charities decided by her family members.

Dr Salima R. Ahmed

President, Pakistan Federation of Business
& Professional Women's Organization

Karachi, 2015

Foreword by John Spiers

Like the book itself, the author of these writings is unique. Considering the vast size of India, writers are all too few; and still less is the proportion of women writers. But, as for Muhammadan women writers, where are they? In this respect, it is probable that Mrs Iqbalunnisa Hussain holds a lonely and courageous place. Here, for the first time, is the voice of a hitherto silent section of Indian women.

As you read what she has to say, on subjects dear to her heart—whether it is the clearing away of religious dogmas and the reassertion of the true Islamic status of womanhood, or the hammering away at age-old social traditions which fetter Indian women, or her eloquent pleas for the means to achieve women's liberation, or education—you will note that her convictions are always based on knowledge, a sound knowledge born out of her own rich experiences.

Apart from that most illuminating account of her introduction to life in an English university town, Mrs Hussain does not tell us much about herself, so a few notes concerning her own life will be of some interest.

She was married when she was fifteen, not a very young age as marriages go in India, and here she had an amazing stroke of good fortune, for Mr Hussain, an official in the service of the Mysore government, encouraged his bride's ambition to know how to read and write in English. Mrs Hussain already knew Urdu and Persian, but her knowledge of English was limited to simple and not always reliable books of the self-taught variety. Now, she had a husband who helped her to study and approved of every step she took to further her education. Sometime after her marriage, she joined a school in Mysore.

Her progress was not impeded by the fact that she had a home and children to look after. Indeed, having so much to do seems to have spurred her on all the more. She earned her BA degree in 1930 from the Maharani's College in Mysore, obtaining a gold medal—a really amazing record for a lady who had been brought up in strict purdah, who knew practically nothing of the great world of education when she was married, and who by this time had seven children! Her eldest son also passed his BA examination two years later. With her son, Mrs Hussain went to England in 1933. That experience, while it was terribly bewildering and startling at first, was also the source of much of the inspiration and drive that encouraged her to turn to the actual work that she realized it was her duty to do.

Early in her career, she became headmistress of a primary school and, after some struggles, managed to get it converted into an Urdu Girls' Middle School, which is now prospering. She also instituted a School of Home Industries for Muslim Women in Bangalore, formed a Teachers' Association for Muslim Lady Teachers, which is still under her presidentship, and, against great opposition from her community, started the Girl Guides Movement among Muslim girls. She later joined the High School and continued her work with increased enthusiasm. In every one of these social efforts, and by her speeches and articles in the Muslim press, her main objective has been to release the women of India, and particularly the women of the Indian Muslim world, from the state of ignorance and quiescent resignation which false tradition has imposed on them. Like all pioneers, she has had to bear the bitter burden of a highly scandalized, critical, and bigoted orthodoxy.

In this respect, not only did she have the joyous experience of flying far outside the bars of the purdah cage, but also the delight of sharing in the freedom of women in Europe, and the stirring example of the freed Muslim women of Turkey. In Istanbul, she represented India at the Twelfth International Women's Congress. Back in India, she is a keen member of the All-India Women's Conferences. She is, at present, in the Mysore Educational Service.

Mrs Hussain is far from being anything approaching the typical reformer. She has a charming manner and a rich sense of humour. Mrs Hussain has set a wonderful example to the women of her community, who generally after marriage think themselves past any possibility of originality and happiness in life. Mrs Hussain is young-spirited and is only at the beginning of a long and useful career. It is my opinion that her public life has hardly begun. Her husband, her children—who are as free as the most modern educational methods in India can make them—and all her wide circle of friends will agree with me here, and will join with me in wishing her the strength and power to carry on the so timely and good work she has so ably shouldered.

Some portions of this book have already appeared in print and acknowledgment is gratefully made to the following journals: *The Deccan Times*, Madras; *The Star of Islam*, Colombo; The *Punjab Review*, Lahore; *Life*, Bangalore; *The Muslim Review*, Lucknow; *The Daily Post*, Bangalore; *The Hurricane*, Lahore; and *The Eastern Times*, Lahore.

As for the book itself, I believe it will be the forerunner of many others from the same pen, and it will undoubtedly prove to be a stimulus to other Muhammadan ladies in India to follow the path that the brave Mrs Hussain has had to tread alone, a path that will be widened and will ultimately lead to the complete emancipation of Indian womanhood.

John Spiers

Bangalore, 1940

Introduction

IQBALUNNISA HUSSAIN: WOMEN, ISLAM, AND TRANSNATIONAL FEMINIST POLITICS IN THE EARLY TWENTIETH CENTURY

In 1940, the Bangalore-based Hosali Press published a collection of essays and speeches called *Changing India: A Muslim Woman Speaks* by a woman named Iqbalunnisa Hussain (1897–1954).[1] Four years later in 1944, the author followed this publication with a novel, *Purdah and Polygamy: Life in an Indian Muslim Household*. Both texts highlight important concerns that were covered by Indian English writing and also addressed by women's organizations such as the Women's Indian Association (WIA) and the All-India Women's Conference (AIWC). Yet neither texts figure in significant edited compendiums of Indian literature, such as Arvind Mehrotra's *An Illustrated History of Indian Literature in English* or Susie Tharu's and K. Lalita's *Women Writing in India: 600 BC to the Present*.[2] In their comments on Indian writing in English in the nineteenth and early-twentieth centuries, Eunice de Souza and Lindsay Pereira refer to the novel *Purdah and Polygamy* as 'virtually forgotten'.[3] Who is 'virtually forgotten' here and why?

The task of recovery, analysis, and criticism of women's writings has been foundational to feminist literary history.[4]

Feminist literary studies have questioned the processes involved in formation of knowledge, including the production of disciplines, the norms of 'canon' formation, and the institutionalization of intellectual criticism.[5] Furthermore, scholarship on non-Western societies has contested the very notion of 'feminism' critiquing the 'naturalizing' tendencies of 'Western' feminism and the marginalization of 'third world women'.[6] The publication of a new edition of *Changing India* and a renewed focus on the writings of Iqbalunnisa Hussain (Iqbalunnisa) constitutes feminist efforts to resist marginalization within academic scholarship and reinterpret past voices for current readership.

Iqbalunnisa's *Changing India* and *Purdah and Polygamy* represent little-known but important engagement with questions of feminist concern in South Asia during the decades of the 1930s and the 1940s involving Islam and relations between the 'East' and the 'West,' childhood and early education, gender inequality, domesticity, and sexual politics in the family. Born in Bangalore in 1897, Iqbalunnisa Hussain was one of seven siblings and her father, Ghulam Mohiuddin, worked as a Superintendent in the colonial police.[7] The family claimed direct descent from Tipu Sultan and Iqbalunnisa's grandmother collected a pension throughout her life because her great grandfather died in the Mysore war against the British.

Iqbalunnisa initially received her education in Urdu, Persian, and Arabic at home and was married at 15 to Syed Ghulam Hussain, an official in the Mysore government.

She continued her education after marriage and completed her BA from Maharani College in Mysore. She had seven children and in 1933 travelled to the UK with one of her sons, Bashir uz-Zaman, to do a Diploma in Education from Leeds University. Following her return from UK, she was actively involved in efforts to promote women's education and wrote frequently for various English dailies. Amongst her children, Salima Ahmed migrated to Karachi after Partition and is the founder and President of Pakistan Federation of Business and Professional Women's Organization.[8] Besides Bashir uz-Zaman, two of her other sons, Wahid uz-Zaman and Rafi uz-Zaman also migrated to England before 1947 and Iqbalunnisa joined them in UK in 1951. She died in UK in 1954 at the age of fifty-seven.

In her reformist efforts, Iqbalunnisa started a middle school for girls, an institute of vocational training for women, and formed a Teachers Association in Bangalore. She was also a member of AIWC and was a delegate from Mysore at the fifth, sixth, and seventh sessions of AIWC held in Lahore (12–16 January 1931), Madras (28 December 1931–1 January 1932), and Lucknow (28 December 1932–1 January 1933) respectively. At the sixth session, she supported a resolution for the welfare of school children involving provision of adequate playgrounds and medical inspection in schools. She also emphasized the introduction of mobile libraries and film screenings in promoting adult education.[9]

TRAVELS TO THE UK

In 1933, Iqbalunnisa embarked on a ship from the city of Colombo to begin her education at University of Leeds in UK. She arrived in England twenty-five days later and was accompanied in her voyage by her eldest son. In making this journey, Iqbalunnisa joined the growing league of Indian women travelling to Britain in increasing numbers since the late nineteenth century. In 1883, Pandita Ramabai travelled to England in an age, when such journeys for upper-caste women were seen as violations of acceptable norms.[10] Within the Muslim community, Ameena Tyabji and Zubeida Futehally from the prominent Tyabji clan were in London in 1894 along with their family. Almost a decade later, in 1906, Atiya Fyzee (1877–1967) travelled to the UK to study at a teacher's training college and recorded details of her stay in a diary that was serialized in the Urdu women's journal, *Tahzib un-Niswan* (Women's Culture) in 1907.[11] Iqbalunnisa's voyage to study at Leeds thus highlights a growing strength of diasporic communities in Britain, and greater cultural exchanges facilitated by connections of colonialism.

In a lecture given to Mysore University on 29 November 1935, Iqbalunnisa briefly described her experiences at University of Leeds. As an autobiographical fragment, the essay is unique because it enacts self-narrative as an oral performance involving an immediate response from its audience instead of a print publication. Iqbalunnisa here says that the thought of attending an educational institution in England started to preoccupy her from 1930, when she got her degree from the University of Mysore. Her desire came to fruition in 1933, when her son decided to leave for England for higher education.[12]

Of her arrival in the UK, she says that 'words lack to describe the thrill of joy we felt on landing in the country which we cherished to visit for a long time'.[13] Her essay then goes on to describe her experiences of the first few days in England and her meetings with various people, including the Secretary of the Indian Association, the Principal of the Women's Section of the Education Department, and the Secretary of the Student Halls. Most of her descriptions involve amicable and congenial conversations with her teachers or the warden either at dinner or a dance. Later in her lecture, she gives details of the university courses, various student societies, and management of student halls, adding that 'I have been dwelling upon these details just to impress upon you the kind of relationship that exists between students and professors in England' and 'how I wish the same atmosphere prevailed here'.[14] Iqbalunnisa's concern with establishing a certain conception of learning, especially in teacher-student relationships, was one of the features of her interest in education, which she internalized at Leeds and advocated later in life.

In addition to her training at Leeds, Iqbalunnisa's activities in Britain also included interaction with institutions and associations established by Muslims settled in Britain in the early twentieth century. In February 1935, she was invited to give a talk before the Muslim Society of Great Britain (MSGB) in London. MSGB was the London offshoot of the

Woking Muslim Mission begun in 1912. In 1889, G. W. Leitner, a former registrar at the University of Punjab in Lahore established a mosque in Woking, with the financial assistance of Shah Jahan Begum of Bhopal.[15] In 1912, Khwaja Kamaluddin, a barrister from Lahore, started the Woking Muslim Mission to consolidate an Islamic presence in Britain. The mission attracted several Indian Muslims who arrived in Britain in greater numbers at the turn of the century. As Ansari has noted, the main goal of the Woking Mission was 'acculturation', where Islamic thought was reinterpreted to make it more conducive to the British environment in order to demonstrate similarities between Islam and Christianity.[16] Their journal, *Islamic Review,* carried views on themes typically close to reformers, especially the position of women in Islam, familial issues such as polygyny, rationalistic theology, and Muslim religious practices.

In her talk, Iqbalunnisa highlighted the importance of women's education with special emphasis on equivalence of temperaments between men and women. Insisting on fundamental similarity between men and women, she argues that 'woman as an individual has the same power of feelings, sentiments, and emotions as a man.'[17] Elaborating her views, she adds 'women are susceptible to the joys and sorrows of this world to the same extent as men.' They, like men continually fall prey to the ills of existence. They have to encounter in the battles of this world the same amount of evil as men. If philosophy is a solace of mind to a man, it is the same to a woman. If he takes interest in literary pursuits she also takes interest as keenly, if she is given the same opportunity and facility.[18]

In these poignant sentences, I argue, Iqbalunnisa articulates a theoretical foundation of 'psycho-social essentialism' between men and women which forms the basis of her views on female education and is also the driving philosophy in her vision of social justice. According to Iqbalunnisa, women have essentially the same emotions, feelings, and instincts as men and thus both deserve education and equal treatment.[19] Drawing on psycho-social essentialism between the sexes, Iqbalunnisa asked her exclusively male audience at the MSGB that 'is it not the greatest delight of we humans to do great services which contribute to the well-being of the whole of humanity...is it right that they (women) should be deprived by men of almost every opportunity of exercising the great powers they possess?'[20] By employing the category of 'humans' and the abstract community of 'the whole of humanity', Iqbalunnisa makes a plea for equal opportunity and constructs a subject amenable to gender equality across differences of culture. Her speech at MSGB is, however, only one part of her larger intellectual framework covered in *Changing India*.

ISLAMIC MODERNISM AND UNIVERSALISM IN *CHANGING INDIA*

Changing India addresses the issue of women's education, gender segregation, and family reform in India through two frameworks: a modernist Islamist perspective that explores changes to Islamic doctrine and practice in light of the principle of *ijtihad*, and a universalist framework that emphasizes the importance of the autonomous individual and proposes an unmarked subject of 'human being' without any reference to religion. Modernist Islam, according to Charles Kurzman, sought to 'reconcile' Islam with 'modern' values such as constitutionalism, scientific investigation, freedom of religious interpretation, nationalism, women's rights, etc. in a way that 'saw the tension between Islamic faith and modern values as a historical accident, not an inherent feature of Islam.'[21] In her interpretation of Islam, Iqbalunnisa distinguishes between 'Islam' which she sees as desirable, and 'Muhammadanism', which is a concoction of the priests, 'a religion created by the priest-class.'[22] It is important to note here that 'Muhammadanism' as a conceptual category had its own history in European scholarship on Islam. Edward Said criticized Gibb's preference for the word 'Muhammadanism' over Islam, arguing that Gibb's claims are 'assertions made about Islam, not on the basis of evidence internal to Islam, but rather on the basis of logic deliberately outside Islam' and that 'no Muslim would call himself a Muhammadan.'[23] Iqbalunnisa's usage, specifically its negative attribution, suggests a complex history of Orientalist terminology on Islam.

For Iqbalunnisa, 'Muhammadanism' is a rigid dogma, upheld by the 'priest-class', where calls for change are considered 'un-Islamic' and 'ideas and certain practices which were relevant several centuries back have to be adopted and strictly followed irrespective of the fact that

the world is changing.'[24] Emphasizing the principle of
ijitihad, she argues that Islam critically affirms independent
judgment and 'recognizes the worth of an individual as
an independent judge of his own self and makes him
responsible for his own actions, good or bad.'[25]

Iqbalunnisa's critique here reflects what Eickelman and
Piscatori have described as the 'fragmentation of sacred
authority' in Muslim politics.[26] Eickelman and Piscatori
note that the authority to interpret, comment, and refute
religious doctrine in the Muslim world rests in the modern
period, not just on some clerics, but on many kinds of
religious scholars, Islamist movements, state bureaucracy,
or traditional leaders resulting in a dynamic competition of
opinions and a 'fragmentation of authority'. Both in South
Asian Islam as well as other forms of Islam, women such
as Iqbalunnisa who advocated interpretations in favour of
social reform also engendered this fragmentation in their
efforts to grapple with modernity in the twentieth century.[27]

The second dominant framework in *Changing India*
demonstrates a strong undercurrent of psychological
reasoning with an emphasis on the development of
individuality. Individualism is the cornerstone of
Iqbalunnisa's psychological approach and she insists that
'the word "I" has its own significance. It is simply an
indivisible object.'[28] Calling individuality of thought and
action as the 'highest aspirations of the human mind', she
identifies 'individuality as the root of everything good and
decent', in which the 'progress of humanity with its culture
and civilization is possible only when the individuality of the

human being is maintained and developed.'[29] Connecting her advocacy for the development of individuality with compassion, she writes that 'the principle on which individuality is developed is respect for the person and a considerate and living treatment of her feelings and pains.'[30] Within Iqbalunnisa's ethical frame of human development, to be deprived of the moral sentiments of compassion and respect was a denial in certain possibilities of human life, a rejection of what life could be.

Iqbalunnisa's specific conception of the 'individual' as a 'human being' enabled her to build a normative view of a good human life based on 'development', involving the cultivation of intellectual, emotional, and social capabilities through education. In her essay, *Character and Education,* she discusses how these human capabilities can be maximized through proper training to establish 'character'. In the formation of character, she included several human capabilities that deserved attention and training, such as reasoning and thinking; creative play; artistic pursuits like music, poetry, and painting; cultivation of virtues such as courtesy, obedience, kindness; and a passion for justice and fairness.[31] Given the range of qualities included here and their relevance for development of character, Iqbalunnisa's views, I argue, emphasize the nourishment of capabilities based on an inherent conception of 'humanness' and also provide the basis for the strand of universalism in her thinking.[32]

What is critical to note here is that Iqbalunnisa's definition of *ijtihad* also relies on a conception of 'individuality' and 'independent judgment', but with the exception that it is clearly marked as 'Islamic' and not 'human'. We thus note an overlap between the theoretical underpinnings of Islamic modernism and universalism, and the distinction mentioned here between the two demonstrates close connections instead of an absolute, dichotomous differentiation.

WOMEN'S SECLUSION AND POLYGYNY

As is evident, Iqbalunnisa was an ardent supporter of women's education, emancipation, and reform of religious tradition. But two issues of gender relations in her writings involving women's seclusion (purdah) and polygyny deserve independent discussion. Not only do they appear repeatedly in her *Changing India* essays, Iqbalunnisa also returned to them separately in 1944 in her work of fiction, *Purdah and Polygamy.* Critiquing seclusion unambiguously, Iqbalunnisa argues that 'it is a serious error to think that a woman who is carefully guarded at all times and checked at every action and thought can lead a successful life and manage her own affairs.'[33] Calling 'man' (i.e. the male) as 'an autocratic ruler with unlimited powers at home', she felt that his poor position outside the home had generated an 'authoritative attitude of commanding influence at home' which 'creates an atmosphere of repression which kills the individuality and initiative among his womenfolk.'[34] She tersely concludes that 'a strong willed husband maintains a weak-willed wife.'[35] The invocation of domination as a trope for explaining seclusion highlights further Iqbalunnisa's categorical stance on purdah. It emerges as a space associated with intellectual and psychological stagnation where women have no opportunity for thought and action.

In her views on purdah, Iqbalunnisa was not alone and is joined by other Muslim women in this period who criticized seclusion. In 1905, Rokeya Sakhawat Hossain (1880–1932) wrote *Sultana's Dream,* a satirical short story set in an utopian location called Ladyland where the secluded social order has been inverted and men stay indoors looking after the home and children whereas the women are in charge of political administration and do not consider men fit for political power.[36] Born in Bengal, Rokeya, one of the leading women writers and educators of the early twentieth century, used her skills in the cause of social reform. As Roushan Jahan points out, *Sultana's Dream* is an act of 'poetic justice' where 'an omnipotent author is punishing men in an ideal world... for their criminal oppression of women in the real world.'[37]

In addition to seclusion, Iqbalunnisa also addressed questions specific to marriage and family. Foremost amongst the practices that she felt were an outcome of 'Muhammadanism', was polygyny. Like several reformers before her, Iqbalunnisa emphasizes that the commanded practice of marriage in the Quran is monogamy, insisting that 'there is no polygamy in Islam'.[38] She believed that polygynous marriages in the past were considered to be solutions for the lack of independence of women. In the absence of an education and improbability of a life without the husband, polygyny was meant to guard women 'from the evils of society, and human catastrophe, to give them shelter, and a respectful livelihood.'[39] With the rise in education and other opportunities for women in the modern period, she felt that polygyny had become 'unnecessary'.[40]

Iqbalbunnisa returned to polygyny again, in 1944, in her novel *Purdah and Polygamy*. The novel centres on marital relationships and the larger patterns of domestic politics in the life of Kabeer, the protagonist, who has multiple marriages to Nazni, Munira, Maghbool, and Noorjahan. Jessica Berman writes that the 'commentary on polygamy in this novel results from Kabeer's endless quest to find the embodiment of a wife who doesn't exist.'[41] Iqbalunnisa's critique of polygyny is part of the wider conversation on polygyny and marriage that took place amongst Muslims beginning from the late nineteenth century. At the fifth All-India Muslim Ladies Conference of 1918 held in Lahore, a resolution was passed that condemned polygyny. The words of the resolution stated:

> In the view of this conference, the progress of the community is hindered deeply by the form of polygyny that is prevalent amongst some classes, and is opposed to the Quranic injunction and the correct principles of Islam. It is the duty of educated women to make efforts to eliminate this custom within their influence.[42]

An address given by Jahanara Shahnawaz at the conference criticized the practice of polygyny as shameful, and the conference called for state legislation to check the growing trend of multiple marriages within the Muslim community. In her autobiography published decades later, Jahanara said that the resolution was passed unanimously and her position led to widespread censure and rebuke from the Muslim community.[43]

Iqbalunnisa's writings in the 1930s and her novel thus converge on a conversation against polygyny that was brewing within the Muslim community in the early twentieth century, and reflect a continued concern with these issues in languages other than Urdu.

POLITICS OF INTERNATIONALISM

Iqbalunnisa's education in the UK in 1933–34 gave her access to a growing network of international organizations that grew rapidly during the interwar years. In October 1934, Iqbalunnisa attended the eighth world conference of the World Association of Girl Guides and Girl Scouts held at Regina Hotel in Adelboden, Switzerland. Girl Guides or 'guiding' as a female counterpart to Boy Scouts or 'scouting' was founded in 1910 and led initially by Agnes Baden-Powell, sister of Robert Baden-Powell, in 1910.[44] During the years of the First World War, the movement expanded to other countries including Canada, USA, and South Africa, and there was a surge in membership as young women were enlisted into wartime services.[45]

Historians have demonstrated how the Girl Scouts redesigned their institutional structure and ideology towards greater international outreach after the end of the First World War. Unlike the pre-war years, a militaristic defence of empire was attenuated and a vision of cooperation and friendship across racial, national, and ethnic boundaries was cultivated to generate bonds of 'sisterhood'.[46] In 1920 at Oxford, the first meeting to formally discuss the growth of guiding in different countries around the world was convened. Biennial meetings were held till 1928, when the World Association of Girl Guides and Girl Scouts was formed with its own secretariat and a world magazine.[47]

Girl guiding in India began in 1911, and was initially open only to children of European descent. The policy was changed in 1916 and Girl Guiding gradually became popular amongst elite Indian women.[48] At the first All-India Women's Conference in 1927, a group of women Guides met other delegates and expressed their support for women's education.[49] A year later, Zimha Lazarus, a delegate from Mysore, proposed a resolution to promote girl guiding on 'Indian lines' and claimed that such activities could also be found in ancient Indian texts.[50] Iqbalunnisa herself was an advocate of the Girl Guides Movement calling it 'the most essential need of education—the development of character, which is the most neglected thing in our country.'[51] At the World Conference, she mentioned the Maharani of Mysore and Maharani of Travancore as enthusiastic supporters of the Girl Guides Movement and described Girl Guides as 'good citizens' who had helped deaf and blind children in school, worked in a children's remand home, promoted hygiene and sanitation, and adult education in villages.[52]

In addition to participation in the Girl Guides Movement, Iqbalunnisa also took par in the internationalism enabled by the women's suffrage movements of Europe and US in the early twentieth century. In 1935, Iqbalunnisa attended the twelfth conference of the International Alliance of Women for Suffrage and Equal Citizenship (IAWSEC) held in Istanbul, Turkey. The International Woman Suffrage Alliance (IWSA) emerged out of the International Council of Women (ICW) in 1904, when national women's suffrage auxiliaries met in Berlin to secure the vote for women.[53] IWSA was formed when German suffragists Lida Gustava Heymann and Anita Augspurg, along with Carrie Chapman Catt, the then president of the US National American Woman Suffrage Association, led the calls for a new organization of suffragists because anti-suffragists had become increasingly vocal within ICW.[54]

The twelfth conference of IAWSEC was held from 18 April 1935 to 25 April 1935 in Istanbul. Turk Kadin Birligi (Turkish Women's Union), the society affiliated with IAW, arranged Istanbul as the location of the conference. The President of the Society, Latife Bekir, secured approval from the Turkish Government for hosting the conference at Yildiz Kozk, a pavilion in the grounds of the former palace of Sultan Abdul Hamid.[55] Emphasizing the importance of the conference, Carrie Chapman Catt, in an interview with the Associated Press, said, 'The fact that the Congress is to assemble in Turkey is of great significance and is a commentary on the advance women have made. There has never before been an international women's meeting in a Muhammadan country.'[56] The non-European countries that had sent their delegations to the congress included Brazil, Ceylon, India, Egypt, Turkey, Syria, Palestine, and Jamaica.[57]

At the Congress, there were three delegates from India including Begum Shareefah Hamid Ali (Begum Hamid Ali), Iqbalunnisa Hussain, and Begum Kamaluddin.[58] Begum Hamid Ali was a delegate from both AIWC and WIA, whereas Iqbalunnisa Hussain was associated with WIA and Begum Kamaluddin with AIWC.[59]

Connections between AIWC and international women's organizations, as illustrated by the Istanbul congress, emerged in the early 1930s. In January 1934, Rajkumari Amrit Kaur, one of the Vice Presidents of AIWC, was appointed as a Liaison Officer between AIWC and various British women's organizations who had supported their demands regarding franchise and their status in the new constitution. In March 1934, Mrs Lankester was appointed in London as another Liaison Officer to act on behalf of AIWC.[60] As a result of the work of the Liaison Group in England, around thirty organizations received news related to the work of the AIWC in India.[61] This effort in transnational relationships formalized further when, in late 1934, Corbett Ashby, then president of the IAWSEC, and Maude Royden were invited as guests to attend the meeting of the yearly AIWC. *Jus Suffragii*, the monthly journal of IAWSEC, praised the two women for accepting the invitation, saying that 'it is significant that both these very busy women have felt so strongly the importance of the conference and the call from the Women's Movement in India that they are giving up pressing personal and public claims in order to be present.'[62]

The twelfth IAWSEC congress passed several resolutions, including one on 'East and West in Cooperation' which stated that:

Whereas this Congress believes that in the interests of true progress, the woman of every country must advance on the lines of equality and justice, it pledges its hearty support to all the women of the West as well as of the East whether they struggle for the eradication of their special legal, social, and economic disabilities and for the recognition of their rights to equal citizenship in their respective national units or whether they are in danger of losing these legal, political, and economic rights which they have achieved.[63]

Following welcome speeches and adoption of a General Declaration of Policy on the first day of the Congress, there was also a special session on 'East and West in Cooperation' chaired by the president of IAWSEC, Corbett Ashby along with Rama Rau from India and Huda Sharawi from Egypt as its discussants.[64] The report of the Congress specifically mentions that 'the session on East and West in Cooperation on the afternoon of 19 April attracted great interest.'[65] At the session, both Iqbalunnisa and Begum Hamid Ali gave speeches, along with other female delegates from Egypt, Algeria, Jamaica, Australia, Syria, and Palestine. In her speech, reproduced in *Changing India,* Iqbalunnisa discusses ways in which the 'East' and the 'West' could overcome their differences and work together for greater harmony. Claiming that the 'East' was not just an 'ancient, unchanging East' but a 'modern East' which had absorbed and assimilated outside influences, she highlighted the role of art especially music in enabling diverse groups to understand each other.[66] In particular, she argued against 'isolationism', stating that 'East' has 'sometimes tried to isolate herself in her past history but isolation has always meant stagnation'. She added that:

> what we ought to realize is that Western civilization is modern, built on the experiences of many centuries in the East and in the West. To turn away from it as if it were something alien or hostile to us is to misread the lessons of history.[67]

Iqbalunnisa's advocacy of greater cooperation between the 'East' and the 'West', and her stance against isolationism points to a politics of 'internationalism' that often found expression at forums of various transnational organizations. Leila Rupp has demonstrated how internationalism within the discourse of several organizations in the twentieth century was a new 'phenomenon and a spirit rather than a formal ideology.'[68] This 'spirit' often coexisted with racial exclusions of international organizations including IAWSEC that remained heavily dominated by North American and European interests, in which women delegates from Asia and Africa had to insist on their autonomy and resist marginalization, exposing tensions in an age of increasing anti-colonial nationalism.[69] In her speech at the panel on 'East-West' relations, Begum Hamid Ali also expressed desire of friendship but added that:

> we of the East must warn you, of the West, that any arrogant assumption of superiority or of patronage on the part of Europe or America, any undue pressure of enforcement of religion or government, or of trade or economic 'spheres

of influence' will alienate Asia and Africa, and with it the womanhood of Asia and Africa.[70]

Although Iqbalunnisa did not mention racism or Western domination in her speech, she was aware of the conflicts at the centre of internationalist politics. Commenting on increasing internationalism, she once wrote that:

> association between nation and nation is growing so close that international problems of a varying nature are arising. Some of them cause friction, no doubt, but some unite the nations to exchange their ideas and ideals.[71]

The International Alliance of Women for Suffrage and Equal Citizenship (IAWSEC) thus struggled with its contradictions, and was caught in a tension between its desire for 'global sisterhood' and beliefs of Western superiority. Weber, for instance, demonstrates how the assumptions about Arab women by the feminist leadership of IAW generated a 'complex mixture of openness and condescension' towards Arab women's movements.[72] Similar conflicts also lay at the heart of the Girl Guides movement with its own ambitions for sisterhood.[73] Before the twentieth century, Burton has examined imperial assumptions about Indian women that underlay British middle-class feminist discourse in the late nineteenth century.[74] Iqbalunnisa Hussain and Begum Hamid Ali thus asserted themselves within transnational networks that weren't always amenable to concerns of Indian women, but nevertheless reflected their aspirations to speak and engage with women beyond the confines of their own ethnicity and participate in a 'spirit of internationalism.'

CONCLUSION

Iqbalunnisa's life and interests illustrate important trends in gender, Islam, and transnational politics during the late colonial period. Women like her actively negotiated and re-articulated religious doctrine to advocate their own vision of Islam and society. These intellectual endeavours did not just involve defining Islamic concepts, but also an engagement with the practices of universalism and non-religious individualism based on an ethic of development of human capabilities. Religious and other strands of thinking were sets of belief that articulated visions of another social order. Both Islamic thought and non-religious liberalism were coterminous with one another. Moreover, movements engaged in transformation of childhood learning, gender roles, and religious framework were not limited to politics within the nation but also involved participation in diasporic communities in the UK and even converged towards patterns of internationalism within feminist organizations. These linkages and encounters do not imply an absence of hegemony or hierarchy, but hint at uneven structures of social transformation. Recovering the voice of Iqbalunnisa Hussain thus demonstrates the transnational nature and multiple locations of colonial modernity along with an intellectual synthesis involving diversity of reasoning and belief.

Dr Asiya Alam,
Louisiana State University, 2015

REFERENCES

PRIMARY SOURCES

Anonymous, 'All-India Women's Conference', *Jus Suffragii*, 291/3 (Dec. 1934), 17.

Anonymous, 'Twelfth Congress: Istanbul, 18–25 April 1935' *Jus Suffragii*, 28/9 (Jun. 1934), 65–6.

Anonymous, 'At the Congress,' *Jus Suffragii*, 29/7 (Apr. 1935), 61.

Ali, Syed M., 'Lahore Ladies Conference', *Tahzib un Niswan*, Number 14, 21 (6 Apr. 1918), 224.

Ali, Begum Shareefah Hamid, *'East and West in Cooperation'*, 1935, IAW papers, Sophia Smith Collection.

Hussain, Iqbalunnisa, *'Women's Rights and Duties as a Citizen'* 1935, IAW papers, Sophia Smith Collection.

_____, *Changing India: A Muslim Woman Speaks* (Bangalore: Hosali Press, 1940).

_____, *Purdah and Polygamy: Life in an Indian Muslim Household* (Bangalore: Hosali Press, 1944).

Program of 12th Congress, Yildiz Kosk, Istanbul, Turkey, 18–25 Apr. 1935, IAW papers, Sophia Smith Collection.

Report of the First All-India Women's Conference on Educational Reform, Poona, 5–8 Jan. 1927.

Report of the Second All-India Women's Conference on Educational Reform, Delhi, 7–10 Feb. 1928.

Report of All India Women's Conference, Sixth Session Madras 28 Dec. 1931–1 Jan. 1932, 58–62.

Report of the Ninth All-India Women's Conference, Karachi, 26 Dec. 1934–3 Jan. 1935.

Report of the Twelfth Congress of International Alliance of Women for Suffrage and Equal Citizenship, Istanbul, 18–24 Apr. 1935, IAW papers, Sophia Smith Collection.

Interview with Carrie Chapman Catt by Annabel Parker McCann for the Associated Press, Jan. 1935, IAW papers, Sophia Smith Collection.

Shahnawaz, Jahan Ara, *Father and Daughter: A Political Autobiography,* (Karachi: Oxford University Press, 2002).

Secondary Sources

Alam, Asiya, 'Polygyny, Family and *Sharafat:* Discourses amongst North Indian Muslims, circa 1870–1918.' *Modern Asian Studies, Vol. 45,* (2011), 631–68.

Alexander, Kristine, 'The Girl Guide Movement and Imperial Internationalism in the 1920s and the 1930s.' *Journal of the History of Childhood and Youth,* 2, 1 (Winter 2009) 39-63. Accessed 29 Oct. 2013, doi: 10.1353/hcy.0.0045.

Ansari, Humayun, *'The Infidel Within': Muslims in Britain since 1800* (London: Hurst and Company, 2003).

Basu, Aparna and Bharati Ray, *Women's Struggle: A History of the All-India Women's Conference 1927–1990* (Delhi: Manohar, 1990).

Berman, Jessica, *Modernist Commitments: Ethics, Politics and Transnational Modernism* (New York: Columbia University Press, 2011).

Burton, Antoinette, *At the Heart of Empire: Indians and the Colonial Encounter in Late Victorian Britain* (Berkeley: University of California Press, 1998).

———, 'The White Woman's Burden: British Feminists and the 'Indian Woman,' 1865-1915.' In *Western Women and Imperialism: Complicity and Resistance* edited by Nupur Chaudhari and Margaret Strobel (Bloomington: Indiana University Press, 1992).

Eickelman, Dale F. and James Piscatori, *Muslim Politics* (Princeton: Princeton University Press, 1996).

Gilbert, Sandra and Susan Gubar, *The Madwoman in the Attic: The Woman Writer and the Nineteenth Century Literary Imagination* (New Haven: Yale University Press, 1979).

Grewal, Inderpal, *Home and Harem: Nation, Gender, Empire and Cultures of Travel* (Durham: Duke University Press, 1996).

Jahan, Roushan, ed., *Sultana's Dream: A Feminist Utopia and Selections from The Secluded Ones: Rokeya Sakhawat Hossain* (New York: Feminist Press, 1988).

Koldony, Annette, *The Land Before Her: The Fantasy and Experience of American Frontiers, 1630–1860* (Chapel Hill: University of North Carolina Press, 1984).

Kurzman, Charles, ed., *Modernist Islam, 1840-1940: A Sourcebook* (New York: Oxford University Press, 2002).

Lambert-Hurley, Siobhan and Sunil Sharma, trans., *Atiya's Journeys: A Muslim Woman from Colonial Bombay to Edwardian Britain* (Delhi: Oxford University Press, 2010).

Majeed, Javed, 'Nature, Hyperbole and the Colonial State: Some Muslim Appropriations of European Modernity in Late-Nineteenth Century Urdu Literature'. In Cooper, Nettler and Mahmoud, eds., *Islam and Modernity: Muslim Intellectuals Respond* (London: I.B Tauris, 1998).

Mehrotra, Arvind, ed., *An Illustrated History of Indian Literature in English* (Delhi: Permanent Black, 2003).

Mohanty, Chandra T., Russo, Ann and Torres, Lourdes, eds., *Third World Women and the Politics of Feminism* (Bloomington: Indiana University Press, 1991).

Moi, Toril, *Sexual Textual Politics: Feminist Literary Theory* (London: Methuen, 1985).

Nussbaum, Martha, 'Social Justice and Universalism: In Defense of an Aristotelian Account of Human Functioning', *Modern Philology*, Vol. 90 (May 1993), 46–73.

Proctor, Tammy M., *Scouting for Girls: A Century of Girl Guides and Girl Scouts* (Santa Barbara: ABC-CLIO, 2009).

———, *On my Honour: Guides and Scouts in Interwar Britain* (Philadelphia: American Philosophical Society, 2002).

Rupp, Leila J., *Worlds of Women: The Making of an International Women's Movement* (Princeton: Princeton University Press, 1998).

Russ, Joanna, *How to Suppress Women's Writing* (London: The Women's Press, 1984).

Said, Edward, *Orientalism* (New York: Pantheon Books, 1978).

Showalter, Elaine, *A Literature of their Own: British Women Novelists from Bronte to Lessing* (Princeton: Princeton University Press, 1977).

Souza, Eunice de and Lindsay Pereira, eds., *Women's Voices: Selections from Nineteenth and Early-Twentieth Century Indian Writings in English* (New Delhi: Oxford University Press, 2002).

Tharu, Susie and K. Lalita, eds., *Women Writing in India: Volume II, The Twentieth Century* (New York: The Feminist Press, 1993).

Warhol-Down, Robyn and Diane Herndl, *Feminism Redux: An Anthology of Literary Theory and Criticism* (New Brunswick: Rutgers University Press, 2009).

Warren, Allen, 'Mothers for the Empire? The Girl Guides Association in Britain, 1909–1939'. In *Making Imperial Mentalities: Socialisation and British Imperialism* edited by J. A. Mangan (Manchester: Manchester University Press, 1990), 96–109.

Weber, Charlotte, 'Unveiling Scheherazade: Feminist Orientalism in the International Alliance of Women, 1911–1950.' *Feminist Studies,* 27.1 (Spring 2001), 125–57.

NOTES

1. In the preparation of this introduction, I am particularly grateful to Iqbalunnisa's daughter, Salima Ahmed for providing me with invaluable information about Iqbalunnisa's life. I am also thankful to Arif Zaman, Iqbalunnisa's grandson, who helped me with details on Iqbalunnisa's family, and remained passionately interested in bringing her voice back to print. For my research, I am indebted to the staff at Smith College libraries in Northampton, Massachusetts, who gave me access to papers of International Alliance of Women.

2. For an exception, see Jessica Berman, *Modernist Commitments: Ethics, Politics, and Transnational Modernism* (New York: Columbia University Press, 2011), 139–77.

3. Eunice de Souza and Lindsay Pereira, eds., *Women's Voices: Selections from Nineteenth and Early-Twentieth Century Indian Writings in English* (New Delhi: Oxford University Press, 2002), xiii.

4. Some examples include Elaine Showalter, *A Literature of their Own: British Women Novelists from Bronte to Lessing* (Princeton: Princeton University Press, 1977);
   Sandra Gilbert and Susan Gubar, *The Madwoman in the Attic: The Woman Writer and the Nineteenth Century Literary Imagination* (New Haven: Yale University Press, 1979);
   Joanna Russ, *How to Suppress Women's Writing* (London: The Women's Press, 1984);
   Annette Koldony, *The Land Before Her: The Fantasy and Experience of American Frontiers, 1630–1860* (Chapel Hill: University of North Carolina Press, 1984);
   Toril Moi, *Sexual Textual Politics: Feminist Literary Theory* (London: Methuen, 1985).

5. See for instance Robyn Warhol-Down and Diane Herndl, *Feminism Redux: An Anthology of Literary Theory and Criticism* (New Brunswick: Rutgers University Press, 2009).

6. Susie Tharu and K. Lalita, eds., *Women Writing in India: Volume Two, The Twentieth Century* (New York: The Feminist Press, 1993),

32–7. See also Mohanty, Russo, and Torres, eds.,*Third World Women and the Politics of Feminism* (Bloomington: Indiana University Press, 1991).

7. This information is based on family interviews and records. Full details of the family are included in the forthcoming article, 'Reform and Transnational Politics in Late Colonial India: Iqbaluunisa Hussain's Islamic Modernism'.

8. For details of her career, see http://www.bpw-international.org/bpw-news/women-of-the-week/1340-woman-of-the-week-76-dr-salima-ahmed

9. Report of All-India Women's Conference, Sixth Session Madras, 28 Dec. 1931–1 Jan. 1932, 58–62.

10. Inderpal Grewal, *Home and Harem: Nation, Gender, Empire and the Cultures of Travel* (Durham: Duke University Press, 1996), 179–229;
Antoinette Burton, *At the Heart of Empire: Indians and the Colonial Encounter in Late Victorian Britain* (Berkeley: University of California Press, 1998), 72–109.

11. Siobhan Lambert-Hurley and Sunil Sharma, trans., *Atiya's Journeys: A Muslim Woman from Colonial Bombay to Edwardian Britain* (Delhi: Oxford University Press, 2010).

12. Iqbalunnisa Hussain, *Changing India: A Muslim Woman Speaks* (Bangalore: Hosali Press, 1940), 152–3.

13. Ibid., 153.

14. Ibid., 158.

15. For full details of the origins and growth of Woking Mission, see Humayun Ansari, *'The Infidel Within': Muslims in Britain since 1800* (London: Hurst and Company, 2003).

16. Ibid., 126–7.

17. Iqbalunnisa Hussain, *Changing India,* 190.

18. Ibid., 190–1.

19. Ibid., 190, 225–6.

20. Ibid., 191.

21. Charles Kurzman, ed., *Modernist Islam, 1840–1940: A Sourcebook* (New York: Oxford University Press, 2002), 4.

22. Iqbalunnisa Hussain, *Changing India,* 2.

23. Edward Said, *Orientalism* (New York: Pantheon Books, 1978), 280.

24. Iqbalunnisa Hussain, *Changing India,* 3.

25. Ibid., 5.

26. Eickelman and Piscatori, *Muslim Politics* (Princeton: Princeton University Press, 1996), 46–88.

27. Javed Majeed, 'Nature, Hyperbole, and the Colonial State: Some Muslim Appropriations of European Modernity in Late-Nineteenth Century Urdu Literature' in Cooper, Nettler and Mahmoud, ed., *Islam and Modernity: Muslim Intellectuals Respond* (London: I.B. Tauris, 1998), 10–37.

28. Iqbalunnisa Hussain, *Changing India,* 227.

29. Ibid., 230.

30. Ibid., 231.

31. Ibid., 201, 206, 207.

32. There are philosophical approaches that emphasize the development of human capabilities as a universal criterion for a good and secure life. See, for example, Martha Nussbaum, 'Social Justice and Universalism: In Defense of an Aristotelian Account of Human Functioning', in *Modern Philology,* Vol. 90 (May 1993), 46–73.

33. Iqbalunnisa Hussain, *Changing India,* 231.

34. Ibid., 21–2.

35. Ibid., 231.

36. See Roushan Jahan, ed., *Sultana's Dream: A Feminist Utopia and Selections from The Secluded Ones: Rokeya Sakhawat Hossain* (New York: Feminist Press, 1988).

37. Ibid., 4.

38. Iqbalunnisa Hussain, *Changing India*, 25, 30. For an illustration of the reformist view on polygyny, see Asiya Alam, 'Polygyny, Family and *Sharafat*: Discourses amongst North Indian Muslims, *circa* 1870–1918', *Modern Asian Studies,* Vol. 45 (2011), 631–68.

39. Iqbalunnisa Hussain, *Changing India,* 113.

40. Ibid., 117.

41. Jessica Berman, *Modernist Commitments: Ethics, Politics and Transnational Modernism* (New York: Columbia University Press, 2011), 172.

42. Syed Mumtaz Ali, 'Lahore Ladies Conference,' *Tahzib un Niswan,* Number 14, Vol. 21 (6 Apr. 1918), 224.

43. Jahan Ara Shahnawaz, *Father and Daughter: A Political Autobiography* (Karachi: Oxford University Press, 2002, reprint) 47–8.

44. For the origins of the Girl Guides Movement, see Tammy M. Proctor, *Scouting for Girls: A Century of Girl Guides and Girl Scouts* (Santa Barbara: ABC-CLIO, 2009), 7–20.

45. Ibid., 25–43.

46. Kristine Alexander, 'The Girl Guides Movement and Imperial Internationalism in the 1920s and the 1930s' in *Journal of the History of Childhood and Youth,* Vol. 2, Number 1 (Winter 2009), 39–63, accessed October 29, 2013, doi: 10.1353/hcy.0.0045; Tammy Proctor, *On my Honour: Guides and Scouts in Interwar Britain* (Philadelphia: American Philosophical Society, 2002), 73–80; Allen Warren, 'Mothers for the Empire? The Girl Guides Association in Britain, 1909–1939' in J. A. Mangan, ed., *Making Imperial Mentalities: Socialisation and British Imperialism* (Manchester: Manchester University Press, 1990), 96–109.

47. Tammy Proctor, *Scouting for Girls,* 25–43.

48. See Kristine Alexander, 'The Girl Guides Movement', in *Journal of the History of Childhood and Youth,* Vol. 2, Number 1 (Winter 2009), 43–4, accessed October 29, 2013, doi: 10.1353/hcy.0.0045.

49. 'Report of the First All-India Women's Conference on Educational Reform, Poona 5–8 Jan. 1927', 23.

50. 'Report of the Second All-India Women's Conference on Educational Reform, Delhi 7–10 Feb. 1928', 34–5.

51. Iqbalunnisa Hussain, *Changing India*, 210.

52. Ibid., 218–21.

53. IWSA changed its name to IAWSEC later in the 1920s and then to International Alliance of Women (IAW) in 1946.

54. Leila J. Rupp, *Worlds of Women: The Making of an International Women's Movement* (Princeton: Princeton University Press, 1998), 3–34.

55. Anonymous, 'Twelfth Congress: Istanbul, 18–25 Apr., 1935', *Jus Suffragii,* Vol. 28, Issue 9 (June 1934), 65–6.

56. 'Interview with Carrie Chapman Catt by Annabel Parker McCann for the Associated Press, Jan. *1935*,' IAW papers, Box 3, Sophia Smith Collection.

57. Anonymous, 'At the Congress,' *Jus Suffragii*, Vol. 29, Issue 7 (Apr. 1935), 61.

58. Shareefah Hamid Ali was treasurer, chairwoman, vice president and president of AIWC. For history of AIWC, see Aparna Basu and Bharati Ray, *Women's Struggle: A History of the All-India Women's Conference, 1927–1990* (Delhi: Manohar, 1990).

59. 'Report of the Twelfth Congress of International Alliance of Women for Suffrage and Equal Citizenship, Istanbul, 18–24 Apr. 1935' 207, IAW papers, Box 2, Sophia Smith Collection.

60. Report of the Ninth All-India Women's Conference, Karachi, 26 Dec. 1934–3 Jan. 1935, 39.

61. Report of the Ninth All-India Women's Conference, Karachi, 26 Dec. 1934–3 Jan. 1935, 43.

62. Anonymous, All-India Women's Conference, *Jus Suffragii*, Vol. 29, Number 3, Dec. 1934, 17.

63. 'Report of the Twelfth Congress of International Alliance of Women for Suffrage and Equal Citizenship, Istanbul, 18–24 Apr. 1935' 19, IAW papers, Box 2, Sophia Smith Collection.

64. Program of 12th Congress, Yildiz Kosk, Istanbul, Turkey, Apr. 18–25 1935, IAW papers, Box 2, Sophia Smith Collection.

65. 'Report of the Twelfth Congress of International Alliance of women for Suffrage and Equal Citizenship, Istanbul, 18–24 Apr. 1935', 15, IAW papers, Box 2, Sophia Smith Collection.

66. Iqbalunnisa Hussain, *Changing India*, 172–3.

67. Ibid., 177.

68. Leila J. Rupp, *Worlds of Women*, 108.

69. For the exclusions of IAWSEC, see Rupp, *Worlds of Women*, 51–81.

70. Begum Hamid Ali, 'East and West in Cooperation,' 1935, IAW papers, Box 3, Sophia Smith Collection.

71. Iqbalunnisa Hussain, *Changing India*, 233.

72. Charlotte Weber, 'Unveiling Scheherazade: Feminist Orientalism in the International Alliance of Women, 1911–1950', *Feminist Studies*, 27, 1 (Spring 2001), 125–57.

73. See Kristine Alexander, 'The Girl Guides Movement and Imperial Internationalism in the 1920s and the 1930s', in *Journal of the History of Childhood and Youth,* Vol. 2, Number 1 (Winter 2009), 39–63, accessed Oct. 29, 2013, doi: 10.1353/hcy.0.0045

74. Antoinette Burton, 'The White Woman's Burden: British Feminists and the 'Indian Woman,' 1865–1915' in Chauduri and Strobel, eds., *Western Women and Imperialism: Complicity and Resistance* (Bloomington: Indiana University Press, 1992), 137–57.

75. Iqbalunnisa Hussain, 'Women's Rights and Duties as a Citizen' IAW papers, 1935, Box 3, Sophia Smith Collection.

Group Photo of 1933–34 Lyddon Hall residents with Iqbalunnisa Hussain, centre, standing, University of Leeds, 1934.
(Reproduced with the permission of Leeds University Library.)

Lyddon Hall, University of Leeds, 1923.
(Reproduced with the permission of Leeds University Library.)

إنا لله وإنا إليه راجعون

In Loving Memory of
Mʀs IQBALUNNISA HUSSAIN
AUTHORESS, EDUCATIONALIST AND
SOCIAL WORKER.
DIED 22nd OCT. 1954. AGED 57.

Tombstone of Iqbalunnisa Hussain
Brookwood Cemetery, Woking, Surrey, UK.
(Courtesy of Arif Zaman)

1

Islam and Muhammadanism

The religion taught by the Quran and its traditions is called Islam. Those who follow it are Muslims. The true Muslim believes in one God and in His Messenger. 'There is no deity but God'. His duty is to worship, love, and adore Him, and to seek protection, guidance, and judgement from Him in order to keep himself healthy, progressive, and helpful to his fellow creatures. A strong belief in one's Creator, Preserver, and Ruler shapes one's course of conduct and leads one to a straight path. It does not matter what name you are called by, what dress you wear, and what system of thought you adopt so long as it is not inconsistent with the idea of one God. Complete cooperation with God and His Messenger enables an individual to understand himself, to be true to himself and to his God in thoughts, words, and deeds. Unity with God, or that of man's soul with the cooperation of the universal soul, enables man to improve his powers— reason, passion, and action. The more he endeavours to obtain them the more he knows his imperfections, but his intellect and the light of God in him help to overpower his limitations. He sees into the heart and reality of life and tries to be good without hope of personal gain. According to the Quran, there is no easy road to heaven. Heaven and

Hell are two attitudes of one's mind. They are conditioned in one's own lifetime. A virtuous life is only possible through the development of an effective and lasting high spiritual motive by inhibiting one's own inward desires, passions, and prejudices. Mankind at this stage surpasses angels in Godliness. 'Ye will be exalted only if ye be faithful Muslims.'

There is no place, in Islam, for priesthood or for any such supernatural human species. Every Muslim is a priest and a layman. 'There is no deity but God. He created the universe and rules it with love and mercy. He alone is to be worshipped; in Him confidence is to be placed in time of adversity.' According to Islam, no class distinction or reverence should be paid to any particular person because he has learnt to read or write. Muslims are 'peasants and farmers, statesmen, and rulers at one and the same time.' Islam advocates the dignity of labour; no work was mean or ignoble in Prophet Muhammad's (PBUH) time. Prophet Muhammad (PBUH) discouraged the pomp and show of wealthy people. The services of Islam towards the emancipation of slaves are a well-known fact. In short, Islam teaches its members to love each other, to be truthful and honest, to help the needy, the poor, the orphans, and to dedicate one's life to the service of mankind.

Muhammadanism is a religion created by the priest-class. They had to make their own living and to make the masses understand the original text (which, being in Arabic, could not be followed by the ordinary illiterate man). Ready-made laws which suited the needs of the human beings of those days were put before them. They could follow them mechanically without any difficulty, and so did not try to know the real principles of Islam. In the absence of real principles, 'The dry bones of religion are nothing, the spirit that quickens the bones is all.'

Muhammadanism lays fixed religious dogmas and sets a rigid, spiritual truth. These are passed from one generation to another, year after year. Any change in them is considered un-Islamic. The ideas and certain practices which were relevant several centuries back have to be adopted and strictly followed irrespective of the fact that the world is changing. Needs and ideas should also change with it. Mechanical adoption of the code of rules has made life easy and has killed intellect. The artificial purdah system observed in the present world was neither advocated, nor was it practised with this rigidity, in the days of the Prophet Muhammad (PBUH). No check was put on a woman's activities so long as she had an idea of self-respect. Drinking of alcohol was prohibited, and the Ramazan [Ramadhan] fast was meant to make people hardy and to teach them self-control. These are so misinterpreted that a person who does not observe them is not called a Muslim.

Polygamy is another concoction of the Muhammadans. It is followed very religiously, without any regard to the conditions on which it was sanctioned. It is given to understand that man, by his protection of a woman, is making her virtuous. Neither modern psychology nor common sense supports this idea. On the other hand, freedom of thought, useful education, health, and character are more powerful factors in making a person virtuous. Praying five times has also its own significance. It has become so mechanical that a person without any idea of thought can pray and hope to go to heaven. 'Words without thought to heaven never go'. A man saying his prayers five times is ever-ready to take a bribe, to tell a lie, to intrigue, to deceive innocent beings. These are things which cannot be seen, so they are not un-Islamic!

Class distinction is so great that people belonging to the so-called lower class are kept at arm's length. It is also very pronounced between the rich and the poor. The doctrine of kismet (fate) reigns everywhere. It has made people inactive, lazy, and fatalistic. A false dignity of position prevails and Muhammad's (PBUH) teaching is neglected. The religion, in the hands of such persons, who pay undue attention to forms and formulas, has been degraded. Consequently religion, Instead of lifting them up has pulled them down; these are the ones whom, the whip alone prevents from doing mischief.

Consequently, one finds in one's daily life that there are sects among Muslims. Differences in opinion, thought, and action have separated them. Indifference to religion, and the impurity of some, has been responsible for the break with the real spirit of Islam, which is the soul. But it is the body that is worshipped. 'Religion has been divorced from life and so the followers of Islam as a nation have decayed.'

2

Ijtihad: The Basic Principle of Islam

It is a universally agreed fact that Islam is the most democratic form of religion, being based on the principle of movement—*Ijtihad*. The word literally means 'exertion with a view to forming an independent judgement on a legal problem'. Islam recognizes the worth of an individual as an independent judge of his own self and makes him responsible for his own actions, good or bad. Hence, punishment for one's wrongdoings is inevitable in Islam. The priesthood, and the confession of one's own guilt, have no place in it. It also recognizes man as a unifying factor in human society, and disapproves of blood relationships and distinctions of caste and creed. It advocates that all human life has a spiritual basis, although it revels in temporal activities. Thus, it does not make any difference between the spiritual and secular domains. This theory is upheld by the principle of *Tawhid* (making one), which lays the foundation of world unity. Islam also recognizes the psychological unity of the human family.

Islam's cultural movement is dynamic, both in views and practice. It professes that worldly life intuitively, sees its own needs, and defines its own ends to meet the necessities of life. And the guidance is necessarily given in prophetic revelation[s]. Islam gives preference to the individual and his needs. Human life, though based on spirituality, reveals itself in variety, progress, and change so that action and motive are not two different entities but one is the result of the other. As the world is changing, constant and gradual progress is only possible when every individual of the human family exerts, understands, and forms an independent judgement on a subject: 'And to those who exert We show our path. Then I will exert to form my own judgement.' The quotations speak volumes for the fact that Islam allows freedom of thought, judgement, and solidarity. The principle of *Ijtihad* developed intellectual power and social conditions, and gave birth to political expansion. Thus, the principle of movement in Islam has been a living factor in the progress of the Islamic world.

One may put a question: why is the progress of the people of such a religion so varying, slow, and slack? The answer is clear. The development of intellect, and that of legal and systematic thought, gave birth to many different movements and schools of thought. Some of them fostered a kind of revolt against the real spirit of the original principles of Islam. Consequently, controversial ideas were produced which could not be understood clearly by one and all. A blind acceptance of some of the ideas and a rejection of the others, an attitude of indifference towards reality, and an atrophy of power of judgement resulted. This attitude obscured the vision of the overwhelming majority of Muslims, where intellectual development slackened and ignorance, superstition, and fatalism predominated, resulting in the decay of moral, social, and physical conditions.

No doubt, social reformers and voluntary social workers arose and spread the fire of their souls throughout the world of Islam. The writings and teachings of such people, to a great extent, gave fresh inspiration and developed the spirit of freedom, and that of right judgement among the members of Islam. The ultimate fate of the people does not depend so much on some writings and preachings, as on the actual development of the worth and power of each individual member of the community. In an organized society, the efficiency of an individual is overlooked. The success and fame of the organization as a whole is steadily kept in view by the workers. Everyone feels absorbed in the ideas of social thought around them and loses their own soul. A superficial reverence for past history, and regard for artificiality and show, was given preference to the effective power to counteract the forces of decay in the members.

Added to this, the Holy Quran, being in Arabic, could not be understood by all. Arabic is almost a foreign language to most Muslims even today. The translation of the Quran was attempted by many, not for inculcating the real principles of Islam in every man, woman, and child but for spreading the message all over the world. Here again, one finds that quantity was given preference over quality. The copies of the Urdu translation, being more expensive than the original, were not available to the average Muslim. So, repetition of the Holy Quran as eloquently as possible, and learning of its verses by heart was kept up very religiously. The recitation of the *Kalima* was the only sign that could differentiate a Muslim from a non-Muslim. Naturally, the mere cramming of the [Holy] Book so rich in ideals and principles, so true to nature, so practicable for adoption by everyone, kept the Muslims in ignorance of their ideals and made them follow those of others. A thorough understanding of the Islamic principles was only possible when its teaching could penetrate the soul of man. This was possible only when the ideas were expressed in one's own mother tongue. Wonders cannot come from mere theoretical teaching.

Both in spiritual and temporal matters, Islam gives equal rights and respect to womanhood. The indiscriminate treatment of women by the average man is a glaring example of the disparity between the theory and the practice of the principles of Islam. The slow and slackening growth of the nation is due to this. It is the woman who educates and trains the child. It is she who inspires ideals in him and develops his character. It is she who guides a man in his emotional, moral, and social activities and teaches him the 'poetry of life'. It is she who repairs his natural defects through her gentleness of manner, persuasive powers, and patience in doing things. Is it right to treat her as a reasonless or despicable being? Why is there this divergence between theory and practice? Is it not because the real spirit of Islam is not understood by the majority of Muslims? Is it not because they are the slaves of customs or hearsay or look-say? Is it not because they lack the power of discrimination? The elevation of the family or the nation is only possible when a woman is treated as an equal to man and given an equal share in the service of the nation and the land. Surely the recognition of her worth is indispensable for the formation of a strong nation, for otherwise it will remain incomplete. It is high time the Muslim passed from the stage of ideology to that of reality.

The present Islamic world is not so disappointing. The world is changing, its environment is rapidly changing, and Muslims are inclined to change too. One feels in a position to note that their vision has broadened and their views become more liberal. Conservatism is gradually disappearing, giving place to new ideas and new values. They have realized that they are backward in the matter of sex equality, economically, and politically. They have begun to realize the causes and effects of this and are craving for opportunities to improve themselves and to elevate the nation. In general, the idea of *Ijtihad* has really gained ground in Muslims. The religious and political thoughts being reinforced by modern philosophers have revaluated their intellectual heritage. It is gratifying to see that they have begun to think collectively, and the interests of the masses is considered an essential factor in national life, as well as a living factor which determines the character and function of all other factors in human life.

What is essential is the keen study of human nature and penetrative thought in prevailing conditions, with the view of providing fresh experiences to reconstruct the Muslim world on real Islamic principles. A clear understanding of the real needs of the nation, and a clear insight into the aims, will energise the workers to cope with the mob. One should not forget the elements of conservatism and the forces that attempt to wipe away the broad human outlook on life. Life is not simple and pure, and the complicated barriers of life cannot be subjected to hard and fast rules. Natural freedom and the spirit of independence cannot be ignored. A logically pure and perfect system cannot be enforced on humanity. One has to try to bring up introspective, self-discerning, and efficient individuals who shall discover progressive factors in life and adapt themselves to life. An idealistic system of revealing truth and facts is not workable. Humanity needs personal examples and practical ways to follow. Islam, being a single and inseparable unity, surely will make its followers the most emancipated people on earth.

3

Prophet Muhammad (PBUH): The Most Modern Thinker

The basic principles of the religion advocated by Muhammad (PBUH), the Prophet, were complete submission to one God, service to mankind, solace of the mind, and empathy towards our environment, and faith in the Creator and in His creations. He not only professed these ideals but put them into actual practice. His religion was purely monotheistic. 'All praise is due to God, who created the Heavens and the Earth and made the darkness and the light.' He made the people believe that goodness is the only goal, and thus differentiated between the idealistic doctrine which holds light and darkness as two co-eternal principles. 'Take not two gods. He is only one God; so of Me alone should you be afraid'. He said that *Shirk* (polytheism) was the gravest sin that a man could commit; it did not in any way diminish the grandeur of the Creator, but lowered the dignity of man. He was created as the lord of creation, therefore he should not worship objects lower than himself. He said 'What! shall I seek for you a deity other than God while He has made you excel all created things?' He laid down the broad basis of faith and recognition of truth in all other religions. 'Say, do you dispute with us about God, and He is our Lord and your Lord and we shall have our deeds, and you shall have your deeds, and we are sincere to Him.'

Muhammad (PBUH) preached peace of mind and of environment. In fact, he aimed at making this world an abode of peace by introducing his doctrine of One Divinity and its parallel doctrine of one humanity. 'Say we believe in that which has been revealed to us and revealed to you and our God and your God is one'. No nobler message could be given to humanity. Nations may differ and fight with each other but they have only one Lord. 'All people are a single nation'. So, the division into nations does not interfere with the vast brotherhood of humanity at all. He also lays down the noble ethical doctrine of repelling evil with good. 'And the recompense of evil is punishment like it but whoever forgives and amends, he shall have his reward from God, for He does not love the unjust'.

The religious doctrine he preached was not distinguished from secular matters. It helped the people to cooperate in most of the affairs of life, without enquiring about each other's religion. Although it was coextensive with life still it was an individual's own affair. It facilitated the followers of other religions to work together in all the great cultural movements. The practical value of its message made not only cooperation possible but it helped to destroy a good many prejudices that stood in the way of human progress. One has, further, to realize that modernity in thought and action, in spiritual, moral, and material outlook as evolved in the present world, is the natural outcome of the basic principles and truth on which Islam was based. It is a widely known fact that the religious experiences and spiritual cravings of Islam have helped the thoughts of the whole world in the past and will do so again in the future.

It is beyond one's own powers of expression to adequately state what a heavy debt of obligation womanhood owes to Muhammad (PBUH). Lifting her from the depth of lowliness, he raised her to a position of dignity, reverence, and equality in due recognition of her chastity and in perfect equality of rights with man. This change was a great blessing to her when one thinks of the prevalent atmosphere which was saturated with contempt for womanhood. Muhammad (PBUH) stands unrivalled in the history of the world for his service to mankind, and particularly to womanhood.

He deemed it right that the development of a nation was possible only when both genders were harmoniously and systematically developed. He gave equality to woman with man. He said that good and righteous women will be given the same position as good and righteous men: 'When we revealed to the mother what was revealed', and again, 'And when the angels said, O, Mary! God has chosen thee and purified thee and chosen thee above the women of the world'. He gave women not only worldly equality but also a spiritual position. He made no difference between man and woman as regards the bestowal of rewards for good deeds: 'I will not waste the work of a worker among you, whether male or female, the one of you being from the other'. He definitely stated that there was no difference between man and woman as morally and spiritually both can rise to the same eminence. Even materially, he made no difference. He said that a woman can earn, inherit, own, and dispose of property, even after her marriage. Her husband has no right to spend it or to transfer it to his name unless she permits him to do so. In the matter of divorce, she enjoys the same rights over her husband as he enjoys over her. He gave a share of the inheritance to widows and allowed the taking of them in marriage. Polygamy was permitted expressly for the purpose of raising the economic, social, and moral conditions of widows and orphans.

Muhammad (PBUH) never prohibited women from going out of their homes for their needs. He allowed them to go to the mosque and offer their prayers in a separate row. They also took part in the field of battle with the army, and looked after the wounded and aided the soldiers in many ways. No occupation was prohibited to them. The only restriction placed on the liberty of women was that they should cover their whole body except the face and hands. It will however be noticed that even this limited restriction on their liberty of movement was meant for their own protection and spiritual advancement. What Muhammad (PBUH) did for Muslim women hundreds of years ago is still far from realization in the case of women of other nationalities. The present feminist movement all over the world speaks well for his forethought and deep penetration into the problem.

Muhammad (PBUH) had realized the good and bad consequences of environmental contact and how this affects character and life. He said that the original nature of man is essentially good: 'every child is born in original purity. It is his parents who make him a Jew, Christian, or an idol worshipper'. The term 'parents' can logically be extended to the general surroundings that determine the early development of the child. No evil visits a man unless his own hands have called for it. He also said that 'man is born with certain individualisms'. Development was only possible if adequate opportunity was provided in one's life on earth. Lack of good care prevents them from reaching perfection.

Manual labour was not despised by Muhammad (PBUH) but was considered a fundamental factor in keeping people physically fit and economically better. A concept of the dignity of labour and its compatibility with intellect and moral conduct was realized by him. He would do all sorts of things with his own hands. He would assist the people in their household duties. No work was too mean for him. He worked alongside his companions when he erected the first mosque at Medina, and when the ditch was dug to fortify against the enemy. He encouraged and personally helped people to take to trade and other occupations. He never despised any work, however humble, notwithstanding the dignity of his position as Prophet and king. He, thus, demonstrated through personal example that man's calling, whether high or low, does not constitute the criterion of his status.

When he began his educational reform there was no education worth its name among the Arabs. He recognized that education, to be effective, must be based upon a sound religious philosophy, an adequate psychology, and a dynamic sociology. This theory is scientifically tested by leading modern educational thinkers. History will vainly turn its pages to point to a parallel of the wholesale educational reform affected by him in those Dark Ages, in the regeneration of the whole of mankind and the advancement of the cause of the poor and the weak. He left the world a rich heritage of profound wisdom which, to this day, commands universal homage. The predominance of reason, and consequently of learning, above all other manifestations of life, was steadily kept in view by him. The superiority of his teachings consisted not only of the possession of a great amount of material knowledge but in its great possibility to explain and coordinate all aspects of human life. History proves beyond any possibility of doubt that no religious reformer has ever given such a stimulus to both religious and secular progress. He often said 'that you may think', 'that you may know'. He added that man is superior to angels. 'The superiority of the learned man over a worshipper is like the superiority of the moon on a night when it is full over all the stars'.

The system of education he designed was to strengthen the will to believe, to discriminate, and to regard oneself as a representative of Islam. Religion and education were taken as two entities essential to one's life. In every mosque, a sort of seminary was attached for those people who devoted their time to the study of religion. The poor prisoners, who could not afford to pay their ransoms but could read and write, were required to teach ten children each. This was considered an ample ransom to secure their liberty for them. He gave preference to learning over the money realized as ransom from people.

His mission was to uproot every moral evil. He abolished all the long prevailing corruption, and gave a distinct tone to the whole fabric of society. At a single stroke, he raised a fallen humanity from the depths of ignominy, purified them of all their evil habits, and imbued them with the pure ways of Islamic life and infused fresh life into them. One striking feature of his reforms is that human equality ruled supreme and no mark of distinction was observed between the peasant and the king. Not only did he enable the weak and despised to wield the sceptre of royal authority, but at the same time he raised them to the highest plane of moral education and made them the torchbearers of learning, at a time when the world was enshrouded in the darkness of ignorance.

The habit of drinking, which was centuries old, was quickly shaken off from the land. He made people believe that Heaven and Hell are not places of enjoyment and suffering to be met with only after death, but that they are realities even here. They begin in this very life. Any action by man leaves its effect upon him as soon as it is done. Every good deed bears fruit and every wicked deed its consequences. Thus, the law of the requital of good and evil came into force.

By the foregoing description, one can easily judge Muhammad's (PBUH) power of understanding, his psychological study of human nature, and his systematic and logical methods of raising the social and economic conditions of the people. His every word and action breathed that modern spirit and thought which is the result of the long struggle of fourteen hundred years. The importance and significance of his ideals and ideas shine all the more in contrast with the conditions prevailing at the time. The whole world was in a fallen state, corruption was rampant, and every nation was far from a state of real civilization.

4

The Causes that Led to the Degeneration of the Muslims

The disparity between the real Islamic theory about womanhood and the actual practice has been one of the causes of the degeneration of Muslims. The Quran gave the name of *Mohsina* to woman, which means she is a 'rocky fortress against Satan, a lighthouse of virtue, and continence that alone can save man from shipwreck while tossing among the strong waves of passion'. Muhammad (PBUH) says woman has like rights with those of man—'the same is due to her as is due from her'. This means she is not inferior to man. She possesses the same faculties of mind, the same tendencies, and aptitudes. The deficiency in one is supplemented and complemented by the other. But, what is her real position in life? What are her social, economic, physical, and intellectual conditions?

Except for the educated and the lucky few who are the wives of elites, the social condition of the rest is most deplorable. It is a well-known fact that the Muslims have no [class-based] society, but one section of men and one of women. Secluded life has made them uncivilized. The problems of conveyance and of purdah arrangements have imprisoned them in the four walls of their homes. Their information and knowledge of world affairs are next to nothing. They are the strict followers of old customs and traditions. These have to be followed in certain ways and on particular dates and months. No change in them is permissible. They have created such an atmosphere at home that a woman following the customs in some other way is not called a true Muslim. False religious principles permeate their lives. Their daily activities are intimately connected with those principles. Many ceremonies are performed with real devotion but without awareness of their significance. In the absence of real religious principles, their belief in the unity of one God is dual. In theory, they believe in the sovereignty of God, but in practice they venerate many saints. Craving of desires from other sources than God is against the real principles of Islam.

The physical condition of the average woman is equally deplorable. The school medical examination and the numbers of patients in various hospitals, reveal the fact that at least 70 per cent of them suffer from some disease or the other. Out of ten women patients suffering from consumption in hospitals, one finds six of them are Muslims. Lack of exercise, fresh air, and nourishment have been the chief causes for such a condition of health. An unhealthy person is an unfit nurse and unsuitable queen in the house. An ignorance of the laws of the hygienic way of living has made them fall an easy prey to infectious diseases. Help from medical sources is often sought too late. Often, the unlucky sufferers are left crippled, deformed, or unfit to do any strenuous work at home.

The chronic poverty of Muslims is proverbial. Their backwardness in social, physical, and intellectual fields is chiefly due to this. Poverty is not only the cause of backwardness but also of misery and evils. The chief cause of the miserable economic condition is the seclusion of womanhood. Man is made responsible to earn single-handed, and to supply all the needs of the parasites at home. Social ceremonies have to be performed. Big gatherings of relations and friends have to be fed. Certain customs and ceremonies in marriages have to be followed strictly. Costly jewellery and clothes have to be bought. Presents have to be made. Often, one finds only one earning member in a family (of 10 to 15 members) while the rest of them have a birthright to sit and eat. Manual occupation is degraded. A false sense of social status prevails at home, which even prevents the male members from taking up any kind of work to earn their living. Earning a living by ladies in the society is abhorred; it is beneath the dignity of the man to allow her to work.

Man is a lover of domination and acquisition. He is an autocratic ruler with unlimited powers at home. His instincts of leadership and of command find a satisfactory outlet among his refugees. His position outside the home often being very low, thus satisfaction of these instincts is not possible. His authoritative attitude of commanding influence at home creates an atmosphere of repression which kills the individuality and initiative among his womenfolk. Lack of confidence in their thoughts and deeds is often found.

Women say that they are unfit to follow intellectual activities which are reserved for men. A great veneration for manhood, the consciousness of one's own deficiencies, lack of experimentation and experiences, and a lack of information and knowledge of the world have been the chief causes for the backward condition of Muslim women. Their depressing conditions have a direct effect on the future generations who have been trained by women. Intellectually, they are dwarves. Their faculties of mind, aptitudes, and tendencies have had no chance to develop. In their actual lives, they are called reasonless beings that are incapable of holding a responsible position. How could they be wise? They are shut off from the modern world and its civilization. They have no opportunity for creative thought and action. Expression of thought is taken to be a great sin. They are made to live a hypocritical life. Naturally, a dual life has made them cunning and shy. Their outlook on life is narrow and degrading. A woman's education means the education of the whole family. She is the teacher of her little ones. Their training, up to the school-going age, depends upon her considerate and sympathetic treatment. She lays the foundations for education and character development, and creates an educational atmosphere at home. In schools, individual attention is not paid and the child's interests, feelings, and aptitude, which need a sympathetic understanding, are uncared for. Home is a place where school education is supplemented, where the child's needs are satisfied. A mother is a teacher whose teaching is accompanied by love and sympathy. The illiterate mothers have been the chief cause for the degeneration of the

Muslims. They, instead of making the children brave, intellectual, healthy, and helpful, taught them idleness, superstition, fatalism, and carelessness.

Emancipation of womanhood is the cry of the day. It is not only professed, but also practised, in actual life by the people of other communities. It is high time our men, in view of the degeneration of the nation, put their best efforts forward to achieve it, and to be more generous and liberal in allowing their womenfolk to take an active part in the educational, social, and economic activities of their community. No nation can be called strong and progressive unless its womenfolk are also strong and progressive.

Regeneration of the Muslim nation is only possible when its women are educated and are efficient and independent. The goal of the young girl's life should not just be marriage, but also efficiency and culture. The contemptuous attitude of the superiority of man and the inferiority of woman should be replaced with equality. Real and good education, based on certain fundamental principles, should be given to women to enable them to realize self-worth and their duty to home and society. Any woman educated on such lines will not stoop to silly and useless social customs. Any effective change in the conditions of women is bound to affect those of men. The regeneration of our nation is possible only when our women become efficient, intelligent, and brave.

5

There is no Polygamy in Islam

The period preceding the advent of the Prophet has been designated the Dark Age. 'Corruption appeared on land and sea'. Corruption was rampant throughout the world. Every nation of the world was, at the time far removed from the state of real civilization, sympathy, and service to humanity. The whole atmosphere was saturated with contempt for womanhood. It was considered a mark of nobility to burn alive a female baby. On hearing of the birth of a daughter, the father felt himself to be in a position of grief and anxiety because he had to put up with social disgrace. He would take his daughter to the desert and hurl the screaming child into a pit. Hence, an explicit agreement was made at the nuptial ceremony that female offspring were to be killed. The mother had to do it in the presence of the members of the family especially invited for this horrible function.

What was the fate of those who were saved from being burned alive? They were regarded merely as articles of exchange. A woman was the chattel of her father, brother, or husband. Like any other animal, she could be bought or sold. She was an integral part of her husband's estate and was inherited by his heirs, who could dispose of her in any way they liked. She had no right to inherit the property of a deceased relative. 'None should inherit but he who smites with the spear'. The system of slavery being predominant, she could be bought or taken prisoner in a war for the use of man. Among the Arabs of the White Nile, a purchased woman was a slave for four days in a week; she was given liberty for two days of the week when she could live an indecent life. A man did not take it as an insult to live with her again and, therefore, both men and women became devoid of the sense of self-respect. Woman being a mere tool in the hands of man, the only purpose that she was supposed to serve was the satisfaction of his animal impulses. They were also regarded as business assets to increase a man's possessions. He could lend his wives, as a gift to young, unmarried men and, by this act he could acquire property, position, and favour. The chief with the largest number of wives could afford the greatest assistance in hunting, industry, and warfare. The economic value of women, undoubtedly, increased the plurality of wives.

Illiteracy among women was proverbial. Being devoid of intellectual development, and being helped and supported throughout life by the male members, they were in a helpless condition. They did not have the efficiency and courage to stand on their own feet, away from the help of their intellectual lord. They were the victims of ignorance, superstition, and many other evils. So, they were sentimental and emotional at the expense of their power to judge or reason. Being swayed by emotion and the heart instead of the intellect, they moulded themselves to any position they could secure in life. Not being able to decide a little matter for themselves, the question of becoming one of several wives was guided by their feelings rather than by their reason or experience.

The instinct of acquisition is very great in human beings and it develops from infancy. Acquisition of territory, property, position, and that of beautiful and rich women follow suit. Men are noted for this instinct of being greedy and covetous. The more beautiful and wealthy the woman they secure, either on the pretext of war or otherwise, the more happy they feel. The institution of the harem system is living proof of the instinct of subjugation and ownership. A man with a big harem was supposed to possess vigour and manliness. He was respected in society for these qualities. It was also believed that polygamy enabled bodily strong men to perpetuate a vigorous nation necessary for the survival of the nation. More wives could produce more children to perform religious or similar ceremonies.

Unlimited polygamy was very common in the pre-Islamic age. The chief causes were the desire to have more children, and to support helpless women and orphans. Ignorance, and the illiteracy of womanhood, and their depressed and debased condition also encouraged polygamy.

Where there were no religious, social, and educational institutions to improve conditions, there rose a reformer and a champion of the women's cause. The debased condition of widows and the helpless condition of orphans were the two chief motives for which he fought and worked wonders. The battle of *Uhud* had wrought havoc among the male population. Many widows and orphans, were left unprotected. No one took notice of the orphans, who simply starved to death. He started an institution and made people contribute towards it. It was called *Baitul Mal* or the Public Treasury. The amount realized thus had to be spent on communal welfare, especially for the helpless. This step was not enough to improve the condition of the orphans, so he asked the Muslims if they would not do justice to the orphans and take them as their own children, in which case they could marry their mothers. 'O People! Be careful of your Lord who created you from a single being and created its mate of the same kind and spread from these two many men and women. Be careful of the ties of relationship'. His chief motive was to bring the women to a status of equality with men. 'Women shall have the same rights over men as men have over them'. 'The best of you is he who treats his wife best'. He gave women an equal position with men, both in worldly and spiritual matters. He laid down a new law of inheritance. 'The male shall have the equal of the portion of two females'. He gave them authority to dispose of their property and earnings as they pleased. 'And give women their dowries as a free gift, but if they of themselves be pleased to give up to you a portion of their dowry then eat it with enjoyment and wholesome result'. Muhammad (PBUH) emphatically said that marriage is not a sale but a contract between two equally sensible persons. When he proclaimed equality of women with men, slavery or in every respect sale in marriage had no meaning. It is a lease where a woman of her own free choice submits herself to a husband for a certain consideration, called *Mehr* (dowry), which is paid or promised, with the condition that she could sever her relationship with him if he did not treat her properly or did not pay her *Mehr* in full.

The following quotations definitely disclose the fact that there was no polygamy in Islam and that monogamy was the rule.

> And if you fear that you cannot act equitably towards orphans, marry such women as seem good to you, two and three and four, but if you fear that you will not do justice (between them) then marry only one—this is more proper that you may not deviate from the right course.

The phrase 'two and three and four' is conditional. 'And if you fear that you cannot act equitably towards orphans marry such women as seem good to you'. The condition is clear and definite. It means 'marry the widow to support her children', so the emphasis is laid on helping the orphans. It also means that those who possess the sense of service to humanity and the spirit of self-sacrifice can help the orphans without marrying the mother. Hence, the conditional sentence by no means infers that men should marry unmarried and wealthy girls in obedience to the phrase, overlooking the first and foremost sentence. The phrase 'two and three and four' means nothing without the previous condition. The latter sentence puts a stop to the polygamous form of marriage. 'If you fear that you will not do justice (between them) then marry only one—this is more proper that you may not deviate from the right course'. This quotation definitely asserts the fact that the proper and right course of marriage in Islam is monogamy. It is physically and morally impossible for an average man to do justice to many wives at the same time, and in the same way. Moral justice, or true regard, can be for one person or thing. If it is divided, it cannot be real. The Prophet Muhammad (PBUH) had a real sentiment for Bibi Khadija (AS). He respected her, consulted with her in all his affairs, and shared his worries with her. She was a source of courage, comfort, consolation, and inspiration to him. He entertained the sadness of her demise to the end of his life. He quoted her ideas and actions as exemplary for the guidance of others.

This can be called the real, true love, and sentiment. This can be called the right course of marriage which the Quran refers to and commands us not to deviate from. Muhammad (PBUH) differentiated between nominal or outward justice and a real one, which is more conducive to happiness. He advocated 'If you fear that you will not do justice, adopt the easy, proper, and right course'. Hence the Quran ordains that the proper and the right course of marriage in Islam is monogamy.

It is high time Muslims realize the correct meaning of the text, and the motive of the Prophet in view of the conditions prevailing then. We have to appreciate the real spirit of the reformer who had to rule the wild and lawless people of that Dark Age. It is high time for them to make a study of the harmful consequences resulting from the plurality of wives, and to make the meaning of the Quranic Law clear to the less intelligent brethren of the community.

6

The Psychological Treatment of Man in Islam

Psychology is the science of nature and helps man to study the human mind and its functions. The mind, according to a psychologist, is an active element in the human body. It is active even when the body is inactive. The study of the mind and the development of its faculties are the only objects of a psychologist's investigation—who says that the development of one's mental faculties needs systematic and sympathetic treatment. Mental development is only possible when there is freedom of thinking and action in different fields of activity. Human nature loves independence, and this should be allowed to a certain extent for the formation of character and personality.

Islam denounces all hard and fast rules, rigid religious dogmas, polytheism, priesthood, and domination of human nature. It makes man the supreme being of all the creations of God. It makes him independent, self-reliant, and self-made. Nothing can dominate him; he, on the other hand, brings all other creations of God under his control. He is expected to dominate and make nature serve his needs. The religious principles and other laws laid down by the Quran are elastic and flexible to suit his needs and circumstances. Islam gives man complete freedom of thought and action, provided his conscience is clear and permits the action. Any sane man is responsible for his good or bad action. His progress in life is dependent upon his own individual efforts and upon the development of his capacities and faculties. The theory of life expounded by Islam is to bring into prominence what is good and original in man, to stimulate evolution in himself, and to help others do the same. 'Those who strive after Us, We show them Our way'. There is no intermediary, according to Islam, between man and God to help him to obtain His favour. Man's right belief in the Quranic principles, and putting them into practice in his daily life, will carry him far throughout the world.

Human nature, according to Islam, is free from all taints of evil, every man being born with the divine element. Human nature is perfect to a certain extent and is inclined to be good. It is capable of unlimited progress. It requires a certain prescribed course, both in mental and physical development up to a certain age. A person is expected to have strong faith in his Creator and His creations.

> Surely the Christians and the Sabaeans, whoever believeth in Allah and the last day and doeth good, they shall have the reward from the Lord and there is no fear for them, neither shall they grieve.

A person is at liberty to hold any independent opinion about this or that thing according to his own way of judgement.

No one has a right to question him. No man is responsible for another's wrong belief.

The theory of Heaven and Hell, described in the Quran, gives us a clear idea of the psychological treatment of man in Islam. Heaven and Hell are two conditions of one's mind in the Here and Hereafter. The condition of the human heart creates Heaven or Hell after death. 'Hasten to protection against sin to your Lord and to a garden the extensiveness of which is as the extensiveness of the heaven and the earth'. According to the Quran, man's emotions and instincts should not be killed or suppressed. Instead, the subordination of them into higher and nobler motives is advocated. The sublimation of animal instincts into noble and creative ones develops one's consciousness: when this is clothed with constructive ability, it creates Heaven. The development of one's faculties to their fruition is called Heaven, and the misuse of them Hell. 'He will indeed be evolved who purifies his soul and he will indeed fail who stains it'. The real evolution meant in the quotation is not the fear of punishment, or the hope of reward, that makes a man live a virtuous life, but the attainment of the true perception of man's higher nature that enables him to see the realities. The condition of one's mind at this stage is called Heaven. The onward, or the backward, progress of the human mind is respectively called 'Heaven' or 'Hell'.

Islam established monotheism, to have strong faith in one God, for the edification of man. He, being the chief creation on earth, is expected to work out the great scheme of creation in cooperation with the Divine Will. The furtherance of the divine flame in man is achieved by putting the scheme into practice in every moment of his life. A person's strong faith in one God prevents him from indefinitely continuing in a retrogressive direction, and saves him from being dominated, first by one influence and then by another. A strong faith in one God helps to develop a strong willpower and a mastery over sentiments for Him, which helps a man sustain effort in any one particular direction. He can hope to successfully stand up to a difficult environment. The stronger that faith in one ideal, the more will it be able to reconcile the conflicting elements, and so confidence in his efforts is developed. Naturally, it leads to onward progress in life.

The acquirement of knowledge and scientific study are given preference to the worship of God. 'A fragment of knowledge is worth more than a hundred prayers'. The scholar's ink is as precious as the martyr's blood. There are signs in this for people who understand, who reflect, who believe, who listen, who ponder, who know, who are religious, and who are patient and grateful. Reason and logic are given preference to religion. The articles of faith are founded on a rational basis, which appeals to the human mind of every degree of culture. The religious principles are in line with the needs of one's daily life.

Man, being a social animal, needs the cooperation of society for his own happiness in life. His needs are many, which make him depend upon others for their satisfaction. The satisfaction of his immediate needs and the self-seeking instinct in him compel him to be selfish and, sometimes, to be cruel to others which causes all the troubles around them. He must try to develop a spirit of self-sacrifice in himself. His dealings with his fellow-beings should be straightforward and sincere. The idea of service, and of being served by others, gave birth to that of the brotherhood of man. A balance between one's wishes and actions is brought about by inhibiting the bad intentions before they appear in action. Man and his progress were the two chief motives [guiding principles] kept steadily in view by the founder of Islam, the most rational, natural, and adaptable religion of man.

7

The Position of Woman in Islam

The advent of Islam is 'a blessing in disguise' for womanhood. Islam raised woman from the most deplorably degraded conditions by giving her equal status and rights as man. The Quran speaks of both the sexes in like terms. The good and righteous women have been given the same position as good and righteous men. The divine revelation, the highest gift of God, is bestowed upon woman: 'As when we revealed to the mother what was revealed'; again: 'And when the angels said, O Mercy! God has chosen thee and purified thee and chosen thee above the women of the world'.

Islam makes no difference between man and woman in the bestowal of rewards for the good he or she does. 'I will not waste the work of a worker among you whether male or female the one of you being from the other', and again: 'And whoever does good whether male or female—they shall not be dealt with a jot unjustly'. 'Whoever does good whether male or female We will certainly make him or her live a happy life and We will certainly give them their reward for what they did'.

Islam is the only world religion of the world that has given equal rights to women in material matters. A woman can earn her living or she can earn to help her husband financially. She inherits property from her parents or from near relations. She owns it. She has every right to dispose of it just as a man has. 'Men shall have the benefit of what they earn and women shall have the benefit of what they earn', says the Quran. Again, 'Men shall have a portion of what the parents and the near relations leave'. But 'if they (i.e. the women) of themselves be pleased to give up to you a portion of it, then eat it with enjoyment, and with wholesome result'. These quotations show what perfect freedom, as regards to her property rights a Muslim woman enjoys.

She has full liberty in the choice of her husband. No early marriage is allowed, and no contract between the parents on her behalf is valid. Her consent is essential if she is married in her minority, by her guardians. She has every right to repudiate it on attaining majority. Man is bound to settle a recognized dowry before he enters into a marriage contract. Her claim to it is kept at the forefront in Islamic law. She receives it before all the creditors and heirs of her deceased husband. After her marriage, she retains her individuality by not assuming her husband's name. Hence, her position is that of an independent co-worker, co-sharer, and a partner of man.

Monogamy is the rule in Islam. Polygamy is only an exception allowed under certain conditions. Frequent wars, which were imposed upon Muhammad (PBUH), had left an overwhelming majority of widows and orphans. The Arabs of those days were guilty of double injustice towards such helpless women and their children. They did not give them or their children a share in the property of their husbands nor did they intend to marry widows being afraid of the responsibility of maintenance; the widows being illiterate were not in a position to earn their livings. They had no property and no other honourable means of support.

Any reformer in such circumstances would have been morally bound to support the weakest of humanity, irrespective of the interests of the members of his sex. Muhammad (PBUH) could not solve the problem of womanhood in any other way in view of the Islamic principles, i.e. an illicit friendship between a man and a woman being strictly prohibited. The only alternative was restricted polygamy which is expressed in the following quotations. These verses are the only authority for the sanction of polygamy in the entire Quran:

> And if you fear that you cannot act equitably towards orphans marry such women as seem good to you, two and three and four, but if you fear that you will not do justice between them, then marry only one—this is more proper that you may not deviate from the right course.

The sanction of polygamy was to raise the position of the destitute.

The purdah system, as enjoined in Islam was also meant to raise the position of woman. The purdah, in the real sense of the word, is not so much physical as it is moral. It is meant to be for the development of the personality and character of the women, to instil a spirit of self-respect and self-control into them. It is also meant to make them brave and patient in facing the ills of the world.

Hence, the Quran allows them to go out of their homes for the satisfaction of their immediate needs. In the days of Muhammad (PBUH) they regularly went to mosques and said their prayers along with the men, standing in a separate row. They helped their husbands in the fields and went with the army, looked after the wounded, and helped the fighters in many ways according to the extent of their capacity. They could even fight the enemy in an emergency. According to the Quran, there is no occupation that is not open to them. They can do anything they deem fit. The only restriction put on their liberty is that they should not have too much familiarity with the members of the other sex. This kind of restriction is even put on man. The seclusion commanded by the Quran is not a drawback on the necessary activities of women but is an instrument towards progress.

Islam is the only religion that gives woman an equal position in material matters and in the moral and spiritual spheres as well. Women belonging to other religions aspire to what Muslim women have been enjoying for the last 1400 years.

8

The Present Condition of Girls
in Islam

The position that man occupies in the home, the social environment, malnutrition, and the lack of physical training have, between them, dwarfed the mental capacity of Muslim girls. To the ordinary observer, physical causes alone are responsible but the student of social conditions finds that a hostile environment breeds a complex of the minds which does not lose its grip on girls even when they grow to womanhood. The solution lies in better home conditions, physical training, and above all in the development of a full and unrestrained personality.

Muslim girls in India have not availed themselves of the best that nature can give, and thus are rather backward in class and of rather low intellectual capacity. The causes are not far to seek. They have not been given adequate physical training and are consequently unable to stand the strain of a hard day's work. Slack habits contracted at home and in an unfriendly environment last through life, taking from them the desire and will for sustained effort, intellectual or otherwise. Bad home conditions and malnutrition have, between them, withheld the strength on which the girls might have drawn for the development of their minds.

Despite the glorious heritage of the past and the wide scope of activity to which Muslim women could address themselves, conditions in India unhappily tend to narrow the intellectual capacity of Muslim women through dwarfing the minds of Muslim girls. The past, the wonderful past of the Muslim civilization with the wide opportunities it opened up for the self-expression of women, is a never-failing fount of inspiration, but rather than drink of it Muslim parents turn their backs upon it. Having for long been denied self-expression, they, in turn, tyrannise over their children and deny them any measure of free, unrestrained growth.

Psychology has opened up a vast ocean of knowledge respecting the workings of the mind; it can be easily shown that the present condition of mental inefficiency of girls in India is due to the improper grasp of psychological issues by their parents. The position that man occupies in the Indian Muslim home is too central, too much like the position that the earth occupied in the medieval cosmogony. Man is so revered by women that free talk, laughter, and free thought, in fact any sign of freedom in his presence, is considered immodest, unlady-like, even disrespectful. Social customs have attached sanctity to him that he can ill sustain, and the general upshot of the ascription of every form of superiority to him has been the creation of an inferiority complex in woman. No small wonder then that the tyranny of man should breed mental inefficiency in women who get their own back by tyrannising over their children.

From the cradle to the grave, the impress of a hostile environment has been set upon the mind of the girls. At home, it is a supreme virtue for them to be silent, to talk only when addressed, and to behave in a 'seemly' fashion. At school, the teachers are so high and mighty, such important constellations, that they must revolve in their own orbits. The girls ape their teachers and, when they grow up, they have no desire for friendly, reasonable intercourse sweetened by the desire for fellowship. There is no free movement between the teachers and the girls whereby the peculiar conditions of each single girl could be discovered and advice given. It is distressing to find that teachers use their authority to instil fear into their hearts and, too often, it happens that the mistakes of the girls are made the occasion for hearty laughter in which the other girls join in. No thought is paid to the sense of burning shame the unfortunate girl suffers, the violent emotions that seethe in her frustrated being. Authority and discipline must not, and cannot, be dispensed with; but, true discipline is always in the interest of the children themselves and should, as far as possible be an inner light that, radiating, conditions all their actions. The true teacher is one who can develop that light, not through 'blows and knocks' but through gentleness.

From the cradle to the grave! After the school life is over, the children are not yet free to develop their minds. The social environment cramps their growth. The father and mother set limits to their children's appreciation of life and life's problems. Always following the path chalked by others, always depending on the men for this, that, and the other; it is no cause for wonder that generations of India's women tread the vicious circle. The girl today finds herself cramped and her vital impulses repressed. The day comes when she is a mother, and the repressed tendencies then find some measure of satisfaction. Warped and sickened with repression, these tendencies have become a travesty of the original and she can only find delight in setting the impress of a starved-out soul on her children. And so goes on the merry-go-round!

It is time that women should bethink themselves of this sorry state and conjecture on how far and whither this will lead them. Courage is required; courage to give to the girls gladly what the mothers had themselves been deprived of. Courage, strength of purpose, and love for those whom mothers caused to be born; they have a supreme duty, a sacred duty, that such children be given every opportunity to develop their minds to the uttermost capacity. Then, indeed, will peace and love and happiness come to reign in a land where, God knows, so little of each is to be found.

9

Purdah and Progress

Abolition of the present purdah system has been the subject of talk nowadays in almost all the ladies' associations. It is often discussed by ladies of other communities and anti-purdah resolutions are passed, but with no satisfactory results.

The outward agitation against purdah is due to the ever-changing environment of the world which has become a big neighbourhood. What is spoken or done in one part of the world is known in every other part in a few hours. Self-realization is found in our own women, and that has given expression to the abolition of the age-long system of purdah, which obviously has been a great hindrance to their activities. They have begun to study the opinions of the different people of the world and have developed a desire to follow the direction in which the world is moving. The heroic acts performed by ladies of other communities, in the interests of womanhood or otherwise, have been the chief incentives among Muslim ladies to discard purdah and follow their example. A microscopic minority of the educated Muslims of the present day condemn this artificial purdah system.

The social customs or systems, as they are called, were inaugurated to provide the wants of the people of the country. Naturally, they were the outcome of the demand arising from the conditions prevailing at the time.

Any system, for that matter, has its advantages and disadvantages too. The advantages of the purdah system are many. It has made our women obedient and loyal wives, devoted mothers, and helpful and considerate sisters. It has kept our girls free from the evils of Western civilization and the disagreeable results of free mixing with members of the other sex. Their sole aim in life is service to the members of the family. Not having any other temptations or distractions, they devote themselves wholeheartedly to the duties of the home.

Religion has given them a right to divorce their husbands if their temperaments do not agree. But, cases of divorce in the community have no comparison with those of other communities that do not observe the purdah system. A Muslim woman sticks to married life for weal or woe. In her opinion, her husband's word is law and he is her *Majazi Khuda* whom she almost worships. Muslim society looks down upon a woman who divorces her husband or vice versa. The life of such a person is considered disrespectful. So, a married Muslim woman is a puppet in the hands of her husband.

The disadvantages of the purdah system—educational, social, economic, and physical—were not as conspicuous in the olden days as they are now. It has made the education of our girls difficult. The percentage of educated Muslim women, in comparison to those of other communities is very low. The number of graduates in the community can be counted on one's fingers.

Socially, Muslim purdah clad women are not taken to be civilized people. They have very few opportunities to mix with the women of other communities who are more civilized. Their experiences of the world are next to nothing.

The financial condition of the community in general needs no description. Its poverty is chronic and proverbial. A Muslim man is expected to earn to provide the needs of home and children, to teach the latter if he is an educated person, and to be an escort to his womenfolk. Hence, our ladies generally are parasites in rich families and an economic burden in poor ones, whereas the women of other communities are a great source of help to men in every sphere of life. Naturally, the financial condition of other communities is much better than ours.

Seclusion has undermined the health of Muslim women. They are physically unfit for any strenuous work. Eighty per cent of the girls of school-going age suffer from some disease or other which can easily be cured by sunlight, fresh air, and exercise. Purdah, along with illiteracy and ignorance has cramped their personalities.

They are not in a position to take care of themselves. Before marriage, the fathers and brothers provide their needs and afterwards it is husbands and sons. Development of personality is acquired by a life of contact with others in daily experiences.

What is the effect of the system on the community, and on the nation at large? It is a well-known fact that the community is far behind in progress. It is rightly called the backward community. We have painfully noticed the degeneration of the great Muslim nation. And, we have also noted the causes that led to it. Women are the educators and instructors of humanity. The foundations of education, and that of character and its development, are laid by them.

A nation's success or its fall is, to a great extent, in their hands. Our illiterate women, with their superstition and ignorance, have produced a degenerate nation which is struggling hard to make both ends meet.

What is the present condition of Muslims? Have they realized the causes that led to the degeneration of the Muslim nation? No, there are still different opinions or thoughts. Some oppose the purdah system, some support it, and some are neutral. The observance of this system being in vogue has made our women blind to its disadvantages. They not only approve of its use but also look down upon those who discard it. In their opinion, virtue and liberty of movement are incompatible.

One should not be pessimistic. The conditions nowadays are not so disappointing. Some of our educated ladies have discarded the purdah and are taking an active part in the regeneration of our nation. The noble work of such pioneer workers has encouraged others.

In such circumstances, the only way to abolish the purdah system is to educate the masses and make them realize its disadvantages; and to eradicate the social evils by imparting true education which will develop their moral courage, instil strength of mind and body in them, enable them to adjust themselves to any circumstances of the world, and devote themselves to the service of home and society.

It is not enough to give freedom to our girls. They should be trained to use it properly. They should be systematically and adequately equipped to develop self-respect and behave accordingly. The abolition of the purdah system has been discussed for ages. It is beyond the power of a few to affect it. It requires the cooperation of the members of both sexes.

Its abolition, by drastic measures, is neither practicable nor advisable. It should be attempted gradually and indirectly by providing chances of useful education and opportunities for vocational education with the aim of improving their material conditions. True education of men, women, and children alone will be the basis for its solution.

10

The Service of Islam to Humanity

Islam, the most liberal and practical religion of man, has
done invaluable service to humanity. Its doctrines and
principles make a universal appeal to one's common
sense and to one's spirit of adventure. Its practicality is
so flexible that one can easily adjust oneself to it under
any circumstances. It does not weigh upon one's life and
progress, but is an incentive and an impetus that makes one
act, judge, and think in every aspect of life. It makes a man
true to God, to himself, and to his fellow beings, in words,
deeds, and thoughts.

The unity of God is the basis upon which great stress is
laid: 'Serve God; you have no God other than Him'; again,
'Say, He, God is One, God is He on whom all depends.
He begets not, nor is He begotten; and none is like Him'.
The doctrine of 'One God' is associated with that of 'One
Humanity', to unite all human beings under one common
element—God. 'Say, O followers of the Book, come to an
equitable proposition between us and you, that we shall
not serve any but God and that we shall not associate aught
with Him, and that some of us shall not take others for
lords besides God'. Hence, Islam requires all nations of the
world to unite and understand one another as all in the

eyes of God are alike. The doctrine of one nation creates a psychological effect in the minds of its followers. It is an incentive in one's progress and advancement. No nation and no man can consider himself to be the favoured one. They may fight and differ with one another, yet they are the children of One Father.

Man is considered to be the Khalifah of God. He is gifted with capabilities and powers to control the rest of God's creation. So, he is given an elevated position in the world and is regarded even above angels. He is made to rule the world, to subdue, and subjugate the forces of nature, and to make the best use of them to satisfy his needs. Hence, man degrades himself if he worships other elements of nature that he conquers. He makes himself unsuitable for the high place bestowed upon him by his Creator. 'And whoever associates anything with God he indeed strays off into a remote error'. This doctrine saves man from committing the greatest sin 'Shirk', which means dualism of the theory of God.

Islam, by its law of requital of good and evil, has fixed the place of man in the world. 'He who has done an atom's weight of good shall see it. And he who has done an atom's weight of evil shall see it'. Every man is made responsible for his good and bad deeds. He will be rewarded and punished accordingly. But, 'Whoever brings good he shall have ten (times) like it and whoever brings evil he shall be recompensed only with the like of it and they shall not be dealt with unjustly'. Again, 'To Him do ascend the goodly words; and the goodly deed, He exalts it; and those who plan evil deeds shall have a severe chastisement, and their plan shall perish'.

The doctrine of uprightness of conduct prescribed by Islam has done no less service to humanity. 'And let not hatred of people incite you to exceed the limits, and help one another in goodness and piety and do not help one another in sin and aggression'. This expressly indicates that a person should not be hostile even to his enemy. It also lays down the noble ethical doctrine of repelling evil with good. This is so practical in life that it does not interfere in the establishment of law and order, and at the same time it repels evil.

The Islamic view of life is unique in itself: 'In the creation of the heavens and the alternation of the night and the day there are surely signs for men of understanding; those who remember God standing and sitting and lying on their sides; and reflect on the creation of the heavens and the earth'. The remembrance of God and the reflection on His creation naturally develops one's mental power and understanding. It increases one's knowledge and powers of observation and reasoning, and it leads to experiment. Hence, the very life of man is the cause of spiritual and material advancement. The remembrance of God does not mean mere utterance of prayers but it implies the realization of the divine light in man. Material advancement is not the hoarding of wealth or the living of a luxurious life, which so engrosses man, but it means a simple life with adherence to truth, righteousness, and the turning of all the faculties of the mind to good use.

According to Islam, death does not bring the life of a man to an end but only opens the door for a higher life. It is said:

> We have created you, why do you not then accept the truth? Have you considered the life-germ? Is it you that creates it or are We the creators? We have ordained death among you and we are not to be overcome, that We may change your attributes and make you grow into what you know not.

Hence, the aim of life is to attain a higher life by progress and advancement. The connection between life in the world and the life after death is clearly expressed in the verse.

> And whosoever desires the Hereafter and strives for it as he ought to strive, and who is a believer, their striving shall be recompensed—and certainly the Hereafter is much superior in respect of degrees and much superior in respect of excellence.

Heaven and Hell are not places of enjoyment or suffering but are two realities or conditions of mind even here, and which are felt according to one's own deeds. An action by man leaves its effect upon him as soon as it is finished. An effect of an evil deed prevents man from doing more evil (unless a person possesses a dead conscience) while a good effect encourages him to act more enthusiastically for further good.

Islam is a religion of hope. Hope is a condition of mind which makes a person attain his object at any cost. It encourages him to put out his best efforts to find out means and ways for achievement. It creates a strong willpower. Man is no doubt given a choice to be good or bad—the doctrine of fatalism has no place in Islam. Man, by his own hand, gets into distress which is the consequence of his evil deeds. God is a judge who cannot be unjust. 'And any mercy encompasses all things'. This clearly means that punishment is a phase of Divine Mercy. It is meant to correct the sinner. Mercy is shown after punishment. This shows that hope is not denied, even to sinners.

The above imperfect treatment of the gist of Islamic tenets and its service to human beings shows that it is a natural religion of man; a religion of truth to which human nature bears ample testimony. It is said, 'Go set thy face upright for religion in the right state—the nature made by God in which He has made men, that is the right religion but most people do not know'. The three fundamental principles of Islam are the unity and the all-comprehensive providence of God, the universality of divine revelation, and the accountability for all actions in a life after death; and these are recognized by all religions and their universal acceptance is positive proof of the very nature of man which bears testimony to their truth. The right principle for getting rid of bondage from sin lies in the words, 'The remembrance of God', which is repeated over and over in the Holy Quran. It is a living belief in divine knowledge, power, and goodness that restrains a man from going astray. The sure knowledge that every evil leads to another, and that there is a supreme Knower who knows what is hidden from the human eye and whose moral law is effective where that of society fails; that He is the source of goodness and mercy through the help of which man can have communion with God—these are powerful restraints upon evil. May this wonderful religion of man give sufficient strength and understanding to its followers to refrain from evil, and to give the aid of their God-given mission to their unfortunate and wretched brothers everywhere.

11

Changing India: Basis of Cultural Relationships and the Case for Communal Award

India was mature in thought before any of the modern nations of the world were born. It has grown further in spite of relapses and has absorbed and assimilated, in its broad river of thought, a good deal of that which comes from all other parts of the world. It is not the ancient Buddhist, Muslim, or Medieval India.

It is, however, the modern India, which is none of these and yet is all of these and many other things besides. India now stands before the world, full of new hopes and aspirations, ready to offer what is hers to give, and to receive what is for others to offer, on the single condition that the offering and the receiving should not be made an occasion for superiority and inferiority or for the domination and subordination of one nation or community over the other.

The old barriers of time and space have been broken down. The old isolations are rapidly disappearing. Villages, hitherto remote and self-contained, are finding themselves in the stream of India's life and thought. Self-realization is found in everyone and intellectual development has given vent to an interchange of ideals and ideas in the interest of all.

People have begun to think collectively, keeping steadily in view the welfare of the whole. A cry is heard everywhere to 'think first as an individual and then as a Muslim or a Hindu'. The ideals, the opinions, and the activities of one part of India are considered vital to every other part. New inter-communal problems are constantly arising and new causes of friction are developing. Great thinkers are of the opinion that if Indians aim at building a nation they must learn to live together in close contact; they must appreciate the contribution to human welfare which every race has made and is making; they must understand the customs, ideals, and cultures of others and seek common interests and purpose in them; thus they must develop.

There is obviously a difference between a unity of thought and a concert of thought. In a concert, the individual notes of thought are not only dissimilar, but must be different, and yet they must all contribute to a common and harmonious effect which can never be attained by unity or uniformity. The thought, the art, the philosophy, the science, and the life of the different peoples of our country, though varying in many respects, have tended to borrow and blend influences from one another beyond national boundaries and have brought uniformity to them to a great extent. Hence, Indians can look forward to a real concert of thought in the India-to-be.

The cultural relationship of Indians, from ancient India to the present day, is full of interest to any dispassionate observer of the country. The great cultural wealth of the Buddhist movement was one of the world's greatest upheavals of spiritual thought. From the beginning of the preaching of that great teacher, the message was intended to be communicated to the whole of humanity. The advent of Islam brought a new vigorous outlook and a great practical experience. In religion, it taught moral fervour, the right of private judgement, and robust common sense. In social life, it preached and practised brotherhood instead of caste.

The unity of thought, from a sociological point of view, among Indians is also interesting. A right understanding of it will go a long way towards cooperation. Looking at the question, from the general point of view, one is entitled to use the term 'socialistic'. It must not be understood to mean that the needs, wishes, and character of the individual are subordinated to those of society. But in general, an individual is supposed to efface itself in order to subserve the needs of the family, the tribe, the caste, the clan, or other aggregates which form the unit of society.

The true inwardness of the human spirit can best be discovered in one's art. The history of art furnishes the best criterion of what people thought and felt in different ages. Art has helped to remove misunderstandings and has enabled diverse groups of various communities to work together for the progress of the human family. The art of music has particularly helped in bringing people together.

Its historical development shows how it has knitted them as one.

Religion plays such an important part in India, yet it has made the followers of different religions work together in all the great cultural movements of the country and cooperates with the larger world in shaping her destiny. In my view, the religion of all thinking beings is the same, however different the philosophy by which they explain their spiritual hopes may be. Once this idea is grasped by everyone, we will be able to work together more efficiently and more effectively for the good of humanity.

A great Persian writer has compared humanity to a human being; if one part of the human body suffers, the pain is felt acutely in all other parts of the anatomy. Human beings are bound by human ties. If a person does not feel for the suffering of others, he does not deserve to be called a human being. If people are true to their human feelings, they are bound to feel sad at the sufferings, and delighted for the success, of others.

What is humanity if not a combination of many small families? Each family has a head, the father, who looks after its members. He supplies the needs of his children, educates them, helps them to get settled in life and stand on their own feet. The weak, aged, and imbecile members of the family are looked after and paid special attention to, not only by himself but also by every member of the house. They feel worried till such people recover their health. Then, they are treated on the same basis as the others.

The leaders of our country are the heads of bigger families or communities. Their duty is the impartial care of all, and special treatment for the weak ones who are called the 'minority' or the 'backward' communities. Their intellectual, economic, social, and political conditions are far behind those of the advanced ones. These conditions have to be improved by paying particular attention to them till they are brought to the same standard as those of the progressive ones. Otherwise, the combination of two unequal sections is disadvantageous to the weaker one.

The aim of our leaders is to improve the above-mentioned conditions of Indians and to give them equal status and rights irrespective of caste, creed, or race. So far as the aim is concerned, all of them agree gloriously but differ in putting the ideal into practise. Some want to treat Indians as a whole human family whose service should be close to every worker's heart. Others differ from this ideal thought and would allow each community to progress individually and develop its own culture, mother tongue, civilization, and cooperate with the rest in matters concerning the nation and the country. To treat Indians as one nation is an ideal yet to be achieved. No doubt, India is progressing. Old ideas are giving place to new ones. But, progress does not come all at once. New ideas do not all materialize at one time. People take their own time to realize these relative values.

In such circumstances, will the religious fanatics of our country ever bear the idea of giving up their religious customs and conventions? Will any ruler be able to effect reformation in this connection? The answer will be an emphatic 'no'. Even the 'imperialistic English rulers' had been afraid of such a venture. The Great Indian Mutiny had frightened them out of their wits. If we are not in a position to interfere in the religious and social affairs of our people, how are we going to abolish the barriers that come in the way of our unity and progress? The only way to do it will be by changing our policy. If the minority communities do not come to the ministers, the latter will have to go to the former. In other words, by welcoming the communal award, by allowing the people to choose their own electorate and representatives, and by ensuring that they understand their political, social, and economic rights are not at stake.

Cooperation with the masses and their education presents unsurmountable difficulties. The majority of any community has its own whims and fancies and due to its ignorance and illiteracy possess susceptible minds and is easily led away by any imposter who happens to have the same mentality and temperament. The communal award has its own advantages. The people belonging to the same community are elected. They understand the needs and necessities of their community. They know how to redress those grievances. Their ways of dealing with the people will neither be drastic nor frightening. The masses will have confidence in the work of their representatives, to a great extent, as the elected members and others belong to the same religion, with a common mother tongue and customs which are the greater unifying factors. Hence there will not be a big divergence between the rulers and the ruled. A sense of responsibility, and a spirit of helpfulness, develops in the representatives. It raises them from their lethargy, indifference, and indolence, which have been the chief causes for their backwardness. The qualifications required for the electorates being very high, only a few may stand a chance of coming in that category. Hence, an overwhelming majority of them will be neglected. The communal award with a separate electorate will give them opportunities to improve. It will be a sort of compulsion placed on them to progress. The only effective and economical instrument of educating the masses is compulsion.

Leaders, being the fathers of the human family, have an uphill task before them. It is not possible for a few representatives of any community to turn out work satisfactory for all. They need the cooperation and help of many representatives from every community. The more the number of workers in a community, the lesser will be the individual responsibility. The less the responsibility, the more effective and efficient will be the nature of the work turned out by them. The responsibility of the leaders will be shared, and more people will come forward to work. The experiences of the last few decades have proved that persons holding high positions are prone to helping the members of their own community. I don't mean to say that there are no people with a strong sense of justice and sympathy for humanity. There are some impartially minded people holding high positions, but their number is not legion. So, the members of the same communities who have the interests of their members at heart will do something substantial for them.

Isolation, for any community, is not good. It means stagnation of progress, whereas cooperation is constructive. There is a tendency among some Indians to seek a new kind of isolation. To encourage this attitude is to plunge that section deeper into the mire. It is a well-known fact that any new movement or liberty is liable to have many shortcomings. What we ought to realize is that the present movement in India is very new. It is still in its infancy. It is the outcome of the attempts and struggles of all Indians over many decades in India and abroad. To turn away from it, as if it were something alien or hostile to the rest of the people of India, is to misread the lessons of history. On the contrary, all Indians ought to welcome, in it, the seeds of progress and all the healthy elements that conquer or subdue the ailment to which every human being falls.

I want the leaders, on their side, to cooperate with the minority communities and to understand their past histories and present aspirations. The task of all lovers of humanity is to study each one of them in their separate settings and phases, and to treat them with impartiality. Most of the strivings of one section of humanity have a message and a meaning in constructing a reasonable and progressive scheme of life for all. For a variety of reasons, false ideas of race or cultural superiority have gained ground. But, on that score, perhaps, no community or nation or country has a right to cast the first stone on the new India-to-be. They should use every agency, political, economic, educational, and social, to prevent false ideas from dominating the intercourse of the people.

There are many frictions and disturbing elements, but if the human mind is true to itself and if the members of the human family are loyal to each other, the human spirit must ultimately conquer as it is meant to do. Unless we do so with serious purpose, we are liable to have our vision narrowed and to obstruct each other's progress.

12

The Position of Women in India

The rights of man have been the subject of debate ever since Paine took his stand against autocracy, but the rights of woman have not received their due recognition, even in Islamic countries. Mere acquiescence to a formula of equality has little value in the absence of social institutions to give effect to such a formula. Public opinion has been weighted against the cause of woman's intellectual emancipation, and the heritage of communal psychology has seen the perpetuation of such inequality. The time has come when India has to acknowledge the tremendous influence women play in the formation of character. Immediate attention has to be given to evolve those institutions that would train women to be worthy of the best traditions of Islam, and that they may rear children worthy of Islam.

Rousseau says, 'Educate women like men and the more they resemble our sex the less power will they have over us.' From time immemorial, it has been considered unnecessary to educate women. No provision had been made for the development of their minds, for the species of instruction that was given to them was but a travesty of the ideals of education. Their power of understanding is consequently slight, and they lack the capacity of quick perception and decision. To them, action comes mechanically, following as they do in the wake of the others. They are denied access to the intellectual world. If they are taken out of their havens, they stand open to external influences helpless, as their minds had found little skilful employment. The sentiments and ideas of more cultivated minds appear ridiculous to them. They are but humble dependents of fathers, husbands, sons, or other male relations.

The position of woman as a wife and a mother is not easy to describe. Motherhood is greatly venerated as a symbol of faithfulness and devotion. She is often spoken of with great respect and is the symbol of nationality, as in the reference to our maternal 'motherland'. Women have a special place in both Hindu and Muslim religions. She, in spite of her many handicaps, has exerted a remarkable influence in the home, not only over her daughters and daughters-in-law, but also over her educated sons. She is supposed to be the conserver of religion and ancient culture and traditions.

No one can deny that one needs systematic training to work in an orderly and coherent manner. In order to be capable of training her children and developing their characters, the mother needs the exactness and system found in education. Reason is needed at every step, and education is the means for developing the powers of thought. Controlling a child's temper, and relating his work in life to the peculiar characteristics of his nature, need the sober and steady eye of reason which the mother now lacks, being invariably carried away by the first gust of passion.

Man is such that he considers a good wife to be the one who gives no opportunity for reproach on the score of her having a masculine behaviour. She is one who preserves her honour free from stain. She abstains from committing sins. She never criticises or finds fault with her husband's whims and fancies. She places implicit faith in him and bows to her tin god. In short her duty is to unquestioningly obey and yield to her lord every moment of her life. How charming all this is! But the effects of such a surrender are indeed harmful, not only on the strength of her own mind but also on the growth of the children entrusted to her care.

Fate however breaks this tie. She is left a widow, perhaps without sufficient provision to live on. The most deplorable feature of her position as a widow is the spurious belief that she was the cause of her husband's death. Among the highest class of Hindus, her head is shaved. She is debarred from participating in religious ceremonies. She is expected to fast and show her penitence every minute of her life. The words of Kalidasa are beautiful but what a picture they paint!

> The moonbeams wander not the moon forsaking
> Where rolls the cloud, the lightning is not far
> Wife follows mate is law of Nature's making
> Yes even among such things as lifeless are

She has to make herself the drudge of the household. It does not require a forceful pen to sketch the domestic miseries, the curses, the sorrows, and the meanness's she has to suffer, the petty tyrannies that gall her existence, till life itself becomes completely unbearable. The natural protector who used to extend his arms on every trifling occasion is now no more. She is left weak and helpless against a hostile world.

The position of women in a polygamous household is little short of physical, mental, and moral degradation. No equality could be expected under such circumstances. The very purpose of marriage is perverted as those endearing charities that flow from personal fidelity to one another and which lend sanctity to the marriage tie, are replaced by jealousy, selfishness, and quarrelsomeness. Such marriages end every domestic virtue essential for peace and love within the home, essential for the growth of mind of their children. It is necessary for a man and woman to lead a life of domestic harmony in order to rear children worthy of Islam. Nature never intended that a man should have more than one wife. Polygamy is supported by religion and is practised on the score that it is conducive to the good life. One wonders if there is no strength of character in man to help him sublimate his instincts.

Modern young women (there are exceptions to every rule), in general, have acquired the follies and superficialities of Western civilization without assimilating its compensating greatness of character. Pleasure is the craving of their minds. They pursue pleasure at the sacrifice of virtue, which is the fruit of thought and religion. Ever-restless and ever-anxious to satisfy one need after another, not only are they unhappy but they prove to be a source of unhappiness to others.

> Women are the fairest gift of God. They are smiling, innocent creatures. Behold them with love and respect. Treat them with tenderness and honour. They are timid and want to be defended. They are frail. O! Do not take advantage of their weakness. Let their fears and blushes endear them. Let their confidence in you never be abused.

One feels anxious to know how far such quotations are rightly understood by the average Indian. How many of them have tried to be worthy of the confidence and the hopes that women entertain of them? How many have rendered unselfish service to helpless women? Until women are given the education they so desperately need, and develop independent powers of thought, the progress and improvement of India will ever suffer. Unless the women of India become brave, thoughtful, and active participators in the educational, social, and political activities of their country, India must ever remain backward. Hope there is, as always there must be. India cannot, for long, deny half her effective population the weapon that she needs for her own national regeneration—education.

13

The Differences Between Muslims and Hindus

The outstanding conviction of Islam is its belief in one God, Who has created man, whose destiny He sways. Muslims are rigid in their monotheism and are bitterly opposed to any form of idolatry—'And your God is one God. There is no God but He. He is Rahman and Raheem'. The Hindus, on the other hand, believe in many gods, goddesses, and their incarnations. Gods representing various powers, such as light, darkness, wealth, learning, water, food, etc. are worshipped and their help is sought.

Islam constitutes a great brotherhood of believers. No one is barred on account of race, caste, or position. The mosque is the house of God, where everyone, whether rich or poor, king or slave, has equal rights and status. According to the Muslims, prayer is sacred as then 'the finite meets the Infinite' in one's feelings and thoughts. Strict silence is to be observed whereby that sense of proximity to the source of life can be best preserved, so music is an abomination near the place of worship. A mosque consists of a simple, plain hall where no pictures or idols are displayed.

THE DIFFERENCES BETWEEN MUSLIMS AND HINDUS 69

The Hindu religion divides humanity into different classes according to race, caste, or position. It lays emphasis on the idea that certain classes of people are fit for learning, certain to rule, certain to do business, and certain to work for others. How absurd is this classification! Of course, it has to be admitted that a certain amount of reform, to unite all Hindus into one class, is increasing. The temple is a place monopolized by the priest-class. Entry, even by the members of the same community, is not easy, let alone the members of other communities. It is decorated with carvings, pictures, and idols. Prayers are accompanied with dancing and music which are strictly prohibited in Islam.

The communities are kept apart, not only by religion but also through specific social customs. There could be little co-mingling: one is a vegetarian and the other is a non-vegetarian. Hence, the dishes prepared are different. The methods of eating and drinking are widely different. A Muslim dare not enter the kitchen or dining room of a Hindu. No eatables, or even water, can be touched by the members of other communities.

The Hindus venerate the cow, the snake, the eagle, and many other animals. They have strong convictions against the taking of life, while Muslims require the sacrifice of animals for religious and other purposes. They require animals for their food, and taking their lives is not considered a sin. They think that God has created animals to supply the needs of man who is supreme in creation. 'He has made the rivers subservient to you, the night and the day, and nature. He gives to you all that you ask'.

Muslim women observe the purdah system. The only male members they see and talk to are father, uncle, brother, and husband. Hindu women do not observe purdah and mix, well-dressed and decorated, with men. Islam is against it. 'Say to the believing women that they cast down their eyes, looks, and not display their ornaments, except what appears thereof and let them wear their head coverings over their bosoms'. When women meet, their own relatives are ordered to cast down their eyes. A display of beauty is strictly forbidden, as a preventive against loose morals which ultimately undermine society.

Further, a Muslim, however poor and illiterate, cannot and will not tolerate any disrespectful treatment towards the womenfolk. Public bathing by women is condemned in Islam—'A woman who takes off her clothes in a place other than her home is disgraceful in the sight of God'. Bathing in public places is a common thing among the Hindus.

The mental differences between the communities are also very striking. Any dispassionate observer of facts will clearly see that there are big differences between their ideas, ideals, and valuations. The resignation of the Congress ministry in seven provinces, on the pretext of obtaining freedom, while the English are engaged in a life and death struggle, and the continuation of the ministry by the Muslims, shows the attitudes of their minds. One is more selfish and thinks of his own interests without caring for the condition of his opponent. The other is an open sort of man, contented with what he gets, being animated by a principle of action—'live and let others live'. He is as straightforward as he is considerate. When he finds his opponent in danger, he 'forgoes his rights and forgives him'.

These differences are the chief ones that have been the cause of friction between the illiterate members of these communities. The modern thinkers feel that they are only man-made barriers and can easily be abolished in the interests of the country. But, how many thinkers are there who are really interested in the country? Egoism is a part of human nature. It compels a person to satisfy his protégés for he is responsible for them. He cannot see them unhappy or miserable, so he has to sacrifice his own interests to keep them happy.

Under present world conditions it takes one's whole lifetime to see to the satisfaction of one's own needs and those of one's family. These needs are not only growing as time goes on, but they are multiplying and becoming more and more complex. This is, perhaps, the main reason why we do not find Indians as interested in the kind of social work seen in other countries, where the masses of men and women either live single lives or, if married, have comparatively small families.

In India, differences will remain, friction will remain, just so long as mass education is not attempted in earnest, just so long as social evils are permitted to flourish, just so long as the spirit of tolerance and of give and take is undeveloped.

These are ideals yet to be achieved, but with immediate and earnest effort, there is hope of seeing that the future generation will be happy, peaceful, and harmonious.

14

The Unemployment Problem and Mysore

In ancient India, manual work and education were not considered mutually exclusive and antagonistic. They were taken as two entities to keep pupils physically fit, morally straight, and mentally awake. The concept of the dignity of manual labour and of its compatibility with intellectual pursuit was kept steadily in view by teachers and parents alike. Teachers used their best influence to keep the manual work of pupils within proper bounds and to make it as educative as possible. Pupils were expected to do things for themselves and not to rely upon others for their necessities of life.

Forest schools or *ashrams* were the centres of education in those days. When the pupils first arrived for admission, they came bearing loads of firewood, symbols of their desire to serve the teacher, the guru. This, however, was more than a symbol for, throughout the course of their study, they were expected not only to look after their own welfare and provide for their daily needs but also to serve the teacher and his family. Manual work was not despised or dissociated from education but was a part of the school discipline and training. Literacy and industry were so related and coordinated that they were considered a reflection of life and as an interest-creating element.

The aim of education in those days was the cultivating of an attitude of obedience and patience, development of the spirit of self-reliance, self-respect, the combating of laziness, the cultivation of thrift, and self-denial in the inculcation of the ideals of service. From the beginning, the pupil's eagerness and sincerity in the pursuit of education was tested by his faithfulness and persistence in doing ordinary, and even menial, tasks. He might be sent to gather fuel in the forest, to bring water from a nearby stream, to tend cattle, to look after the garden, to glean corn, or even to beg for food in the neighbouring village.

Thus, pupils were encouraged to take up regular industries and, for these services, they received financial help towards the cost of their food. The pupils paid nothing to the guru for their education which was supposed to be free. The attitude of the guru, towards his pupils, was fatherly and there used to be an intimate and parental relationship between the teacher and the taught.

Now, India stands at the crossroads. Some of her people are abruptly heading away from the natural line of their physical, mental, and moral development, while some are turning with equal abruptness back from it in the direction of the past. The pursuit of the former has led to the loss of their own individuality, 'to a sterilization of her particular genius, a mere mimic of other peoples; a murmur without a soul'. Pursuit of the other has only led them away from progress towards stagnation and has prevented them from assuming their rightful place amongst the progressive nations of the world. Some of them are no doubt aware of this catastrophe and are regulating their activities and their attitudes towards progress. They are taking an active part in inspiring their unfortunate brethren towards a useful end. But, such people are only a microscopic minority.

The curse of unemployment is not only found among the educated classes but also among the illiterate. The struggle for existence, to earn a living wage, is growing keener and keener daily, yet people have not understood why this is so.

Every parent, while educating his sons and daughters, expects them to be prospective government servants. The young hopefuls, being brought up in that atmosphere, naturally aspire to become high officials of their country. But, services are limited. On passing out of schools and colleges, most of them are left adrift on the vast sea of life, 'sail less and rudderless' and without any sense of direction. Many of them, it is well-known, when they know not what else to do and can continue no longer, swell the ranks of that unemployed and unemployable which is knocking at the door of the government for services as there is no other alternative. Unfortunately, the number of unemployed person's increases in geometrical ratio while that of services increases in arithmetical ratio.

Naturally, the expectations of the parents and young men outstrip the demand for work. The result is that the government and its organizations are scrutinized and condemned outright.

The success of any government, or its organization, is judged not only by the number of jobs they create but also by their efforts in providing a living for every person in the country. Thus, the government is the only channel and the only source responsible for the improvement of the material conditions of the people. After all, there can only be a few people in the government, even supposing the government is a gold mine where everyone has the same right to dig its gold. Can a mine afford to accommodate all the people to dig its product at the same time? The answer will be an emphatic 'no'. It can afford to employ only a certain number at a time, according to the capacity and ability of its workers. So is the case with the government. It is beyond the power of any government to be responsible for all the people in the country. The disparity between the expectations of the people, and the actual practise, has been given expression to through several responsible associations on various occasions. One has to discover the extent of this divergence, the causes that make for it, and how far and by what means it can be remedied.

The causes that lead to unemployment are social, educational, and physical. The first, and the predominant one, is the attitude of people towards manual labour. The high castes and the educated people regard it as degrading, or at least that part of it in which they are not directly concerned. It is this belief which has contributed to the preponderance of clerks and teachers and has influenced the classification of landowners, cultivators, wage earners, carpenters, weavers, shoemakers, and so on, and has directed the people towards other types of work than the one which they considered undignified. Another persistent belief is that certain industries, such as keeping of poultry, breeding of cattle, dairy farming, leather tanning, fish mongering, etc. are almost defiling. Closely connected to this is the feeling that one should not do one's own simple ordinary repairs which require a little skill. So, an artisan will be called rather than attempt to do the work oneself. The same principle applies to servants for various types of work, and to the idea of securing as much help as possible and the lessening of one's own industry.

Another impressive characteristic is the patient resignation with which the people shoulder their burdens and carry on their struggles. This is due to their religious philosophy which has its weak points. It prevents the people from taking part in looking for jobs. Along with this is the communal spirit, the willingness to pool their fortunes and to work cooperatively, and to stand or fall together as a family, to combine efforts and funds for a common end. Thus, they have become so accustomed to disease and suffering that they take it all as a matter of course. This attitude is augmented by a fatalistic philosophy that if people are to suffer they will suffer anyway, which has made them wonderfully unpractical.

The Muslim belief is that all that occurs is God's will and all things are predestined. This attitude of fatalism rules supreme in the average Muslim's life and often serves not only as an expectation of events but as an excuse for lack of enterprise.

So long as these conceptions prevail, it is difficult to see how the number of unemployed will decrease and how the economic status of Indians will improve.

The educational system of our country is also responsible, to a certain extent, for the increase in the number of unemployed persons. The aim of the authorities, as all of us know, in imparting an English education to the people was to produce a certain number of clerks—which then necessitated the production of teachers. The professions in those days needed no practical initiative. The present world is full of activities where mere theory does not count for much. Hence, the system has proved inadequate to supply the needs of the people. Once the question was asked: why is modern education so narrow in its outlook? The answer was 'Because it is all done within the four walls of a class room.' Much of knowledge is 'hearsay' and 'book say' and much time is wasted in doing nothing. The working days of a school year are about 193 to 195 days.

The long vacations of Dussehra, Christmas, and summer are times of idling in the name of well-deserved rest. The want of 'practicalism' in the education system has psychological and physiological effects on the activities of the pupils. If manual labour is designed to fill up their leisure and give them training in constructive work, this wrong notion of manual labour being 'degrading' will gradually disappear from both the pupils' and parents' minds. Another cause is the preference given to outward show at the cost of real merit. Our students, 95 per cent of them, pass examinations because they are desirous of adding letters to their names, which will be a passport for getting 'decent and respectable jobs'. Many a young man has wasted his energy, time, and money in waiting for a respectable job and thus swelled the ranks of the unemployed. Western civilization, as it is indiscriminately imitated in our country, is also responsible to a certain extent for the excess of the unemployable crowd. Machines, cars, and other conveniences have thrown hundreds of men out of jobs and have killed their individuality and spirit of enterprise.

To come to the particular, i.e. what has Mysore done to solve the problem of unemployment, one is entitled to say that she has made wonderful strides in the right direction during the past ten years.

One must have patience and a spirit of cooperation with the workers to understand the motto 'Rome was not built in a day'. The Maharaja who is truly a great and lovable personality and his distinguished Diwan, Sir Mirza Ismail, have realized the fact that the great need of the country is industrial training, partly for the development of the country but more urgently for the self-development of the people. They train the people not only for the capacity to have a livelihood but also for their capacity to enjoy life.

The real wealth of a nation consists both in its material development and in the true well-being and happiness of its men and women.

To improve the economic conditions of the people, different types of industries have been started. Large amounts of money have been spent for industrial purposes and for the management of state industries. The Department of Industries and Commerce controls industrial and technical education, the development of hand weaving and spinning, the government's sugar, soap, lac, and electric factories, the industrial workshop, the silk weaving factory, the bitumen plant, and the famous Bhadravathi steel and iron works. It has also forged ahead in rural reconstruction. A number of dams have been built for irrigation purposes and some of the famous ones are the Krishnarajsagar, Tippagondanahalli, Morcounhalli, and Shimshapur. It is a matter of great happiness to see the barren villages being converted into beautiful towns in a very short time. One finds lovely new model buildings there, both for the officials and coolies. New schools, hospitals, beautiful roads, parks, and circles have sprung up all over the state. The number of people employed to work on these industrial and rural enterprises is enormous. It has solved, to a great extent, the problem of unemployment among the illiterates of the country. Educational efforts in the same direction are as follows.

For a long time, Mysore has boasted of its own university. There are four big colleges in arts and science, two for men and two for women. The number of high schools both for boys and girls exceeds that of any other state. Middle schools are springing up like mushrooms. The primary schools are too numerous to mention. In each locality, at a distance of two furlongs, there are four schools: two for Muslim boys and girls and two for Hindu boys and girls. In the city areas, the number of private and grant-in-aid schools comes to several hundred in the state. Great attention is paid to languages both classical and modern. Debates and essay competitions in high schools and colleges are held every year. Deserving candidates are awarded medals and trophies. Education, right from the primary to the college level, is almost free in our state. The modern educationists thought that the levying of fees, at least at the high school level, would make the pupils pay more attention to their studies. Hence, very recently, the government began to charge fees in high schools. Fifty per cent of the students in each class are educated free of cost. There are different kinds of scholarships—government, communal, military, and backward class. Leaving a margin for scholarships and freeships in each class of fifty students, only ten pay the full fees which are almost nothing if compared to those in European schools.

Muslim girls enjoy free education and a conveyance allowance in high schools and colleges. In middle and primary schools, both teachers and the taught are provided with conveyance by the government. The far-sighted ruler and his government have provided every facility for the education of their subjects. Industrial and vocational schools enable the students to take to different careers according to their aptitude. Thus, the problem of the educated class is being solved.

The power of an organized religion is formidable in uniting the people, and in leading them towards a definite end. It is a polar guide that leads a man in the dark.

The Maharaja and his Diwan are the most religious persons in the state. His Highness is called the living saint, 'Raja Rishi'. He is a wonderful signpost of religion and never seeks to interfere in the religion of his subjects, but directly and indirectly inspires them towards a noble end. One will find his Diwan in almost all the sacred places of religion: in a church, temple, or mosque. His noticeable features are simplicity, a true balance of head and heart, and strikingly wonderful patience in dealing with the affairs of the state. His regard for all religions and traditions made him sanction lakhs of rupees for the repairs and upkeep of old temples, some of which were in the most deplorable condition when he attained his post. The priests of different temples praise him in very generous terms and say, that though he does not belong to the same community he is very considerate and liberal in sanctioning allowances for their upkeep.

Indeed, I can without any hesitation state that he is the best administrator Mysore has ever produced.

His Highness and the Diwan are lovers of beauty. Their desire for erecting beautiful buildings, parks, and gardens has a definite purpose. Some entertain an idea that beauty is only a matter of convention and fashion and hence superfluous, but surely it is more than that—something beyond ourselves, something absolute which we can discern if we will. Plato said that to train people to discern the power of beauty 'we require to be trained from our earliest youth to feel pleasure and pain at the right things.' True education is just that.

An indirect attempt is being made to abolish the idea of untouchability in building great edifices like town halls, municipal buildings, and other similar institutions. Around the magnificent fountains in the parks, the rich, the poor, and the beggars gather without any distinction. Each enjoys the sights according to his taste and intellect.

These aesthetic efforts have done a great service to Muslim women who are locked up the whole day in semi-prisons. In the night, many of them regularly come out to these parks and enjoy themselves. It is a matter of great gratification to see the sickly, crippled, and consumptive Muslim around the fountains, happy, cheerful, and active.

One who has sympathy for humanity will be ever grateful to our noble and all-sympathetic ruler. Thus, we see that the maharaja and his government, through their untiring zeal and works, have made the state a fairyland, outstanding in its beauty—'the garden city of India'. Educational, economic, and social improvements are equally outstanding and quite distinct from those of other countries. The praise of the city of Mysore is sung not only in India but also abroad. Once,

Lady Astor MP asked me who had made Mysore so popular. Every Member of Parliament mentions the name of Mysore with admiration and quotes it as a model. I replied that the Maharaja and his Diwan were the prime and moving spirits in Mysore's advancement. Similar questions were asked of me in Egypt, Switzerland, Turkey, and Greece. In a letter dated 28 January 1938, Madam C. De Posch, Secretary of the International Women's Association, Budapest, wrote, 'we hope to meet you at the third International Women's Week Congress in July in Budapest. We are interested in you because you belong to a very well-known State.' There is no doubt that Mysore is going to live up to her reputation as her improvement and progress are not superficial and temporary, but lasting and constructive.

15

Beggary in India

It is an admitted fact that the beggar problem is a world problem. It is the common blight, or curse, of every country whether rich or poor, free or dependent. There is no country or nation in the world which has produced only strong healthy men and women. Beggary in India has social, religious, and spiritual significance. It is sanctioned by religion and approved by society. Because it has religious sanction, it has been sustained and even encouraged from the time humanity came into existence. The weak, the old, the imbecile, and the idle people of each caste were considered part and parcel of the responsibilities of strong, wealthy, and hard-working personages. The latter were morally bound to feed and support the former throughout their lives. It is considered the duty of the rich towards the poor.

The spiritual aspect of beggary is very interesting to note. It indicates a person's spirit of self-sacrifice and that of contentment. Those who have practised these virtues are supposed to be sacred beings. They have to be revered, respected, and their commands obeyed implicitly. Their demands have to be met ungrudgingly. Their needs should not be neglected and should be supplied as enthusiastically as one's own. Their wrath is to be dreaded as it is in no way less effective than that of God. It is also believed that God, being everywhere, presents Himself at the door of the rich in disguise to test the person's character and his love for humanity.

Such conventions naturally frightened the rich out of their wits, who set apart a certain portion of their wealth for the help of fakirs, priests, and pujaris. They were supposed not to earn but to live off the earnings of others. They commanded a specific share by way of presents at marriages and religious or other ceremonies. Social reformers of different religions started several associations for the purpose of maintaining such parasites. Well-to-do people had to contribute liberally towards them. The amount thus realized was used to maintaining the beggars and their families. Such beliefs and facilities increased the number of beggars by leaps and bounds. There came many imposters with some excuse or other. They prevailed not only upon the people but also upon the state, which made great provision for their maintenance. They have been paid heavily to maintain the honour of their creed and to make a show of their knowledge. The huge processions of their congregations are very common even today.

The idea of supporting beggars was steadily kept in view by everyone, with no idea of educating or employing them in service, or to make use of their natural faculties, has been thought of. The false belief was prevalent everywhere that only a certain section of humanity was fit to be educated and certain to work. Schools were opened for such lucky beings; there was, and is, no admission to the people of other communities, nor have any separate schools been provided for them. Thus, their bodies have been built up at the cost of their brains. They are mentally dwarfed and as innocent as children. So far as intellectual activities are concerned, complete ignorance of the conditions of the world, and that of their country, has made them fatalists. They abhor change and progress and have no sense of responsibility. Their life is a life of ease and contentment. What is necessary to them is their care and attempt to secure at least one meal a day. The thought of the next meal is supposed to eliminate oneself from God's grace and not to have trust in Him. Punctuality and a sense of duty are the outcome of discipline, introspection, and retrospection. In a life of irregularity and irresponsibility, these ideals have no place.

What has been the result of all these customs? As a sequel to the indiscriminate treatment of humanity, the number of beggars grew rapidly beyond calculation. The economic condition of the people, on account of wars and many other reasons has not been good. The needs of the people grew more and more due to modern progress. Hence, they could not spare enough money to support the unwieldy population of the beggars. Poverty gave birth to immorality, wickedness, and many vices. Natural consequences were the spread of infectious diseases, and heavy death and birth rates.

What is the relationship between the microscopic educated classes and the overwhelming majority of the poor classes? There is a high gap and a big cleavage between them. The ideas and principles and ways of living of the former are quite different from those of the latter. They abhor and condemn the society of each other as they cannot possibly take interest in one another's company. In such circumstances, it is too much to expect any substantial help from an educated man towards his unfortunate fellow beings. A worker should feel and think like the people with whom he works. He must bring himself to their level of understanding and should study their needs and try to supply them adequately. Then alone will he be able to do some effective work for them.

The above-mentioned circumstances were the chief causes for the increase in the overwhelming majority of beggars and their miserable conditions. So long as the beggar population was controllable, their conditions were not so repulsive and dangerous. The social and religious reformers had no forethought of the consequences, no idea of their personal progress.

To think that beggars are only found in India, as this is a slave country, is to express our ignorance of the conditions prevailing in the whole world. There are beggars everywhere with varying conditions. The condition of the Indian beggars may be worse, but it is due to nothing but the negligence of the heartless people of the country. One cannot put the whole blame on one particular organization, the government or any such other organization. It is a subject encouraged from time immemorial and associated with everyone. Hence, it is the duty of one and all to put their best efforts and heads together to solve the problem.

Its solution is not as easy as we imagine. One needs moral courage, moral character, and the spirit of self-sacrifice as well as some systematic and satisfactory cooperation of the people with authority. A real spirit of work is indispensable. Formation of committees, associations, and laws and regulations should be thought of. Philanthropic workers should come forward, and internationally-minded rich people should offer financial help. A common scheme for the financial, educational, industrial, and physical progress of the beggars should be made. People responsible for the work should see that it is carried out satisfactorily. Mere lip service, on the pretext of sympathy, is not enough and will certainly not work wonders.

16

Is the Present Dowry
System Justified?

Western civilization has multiplied human needs. Environment is constantly changing, and so also are the needs. Every New Year brings new fashions that bring new needs in its fold. Old needs seem useless. New ones have to be adopted and be satisfied. The standard of life is growing higher. Luxuries of life, enjoyed by the rich, are indiscriminately imitated by the poor at the sacrifice of their immediate needs. False pride in an outward show, at the cost of real merit and at the expense of daily necessities, is steadily kept in view and practised by one and all. Religious festivals have to take place, sacred places have to be visited, and marriages have to be performed with grandeur. Costly jewellery and clothes have to be bought, grand presents have to be made, huge processions of furniture and utensils, as well as bridal processions have to be arranged, and several hundreds of guests have to be fed for days. All these mean money. A spirit of rivalry and excellence is found while performing every detail of the above-mentioned items. Women are more vain on such occasions than men.

The theoretical education given to young men and the limited number of government appointments have increased the number of unemployed. They are left adrift, not knowing what to do after completing their education. Their immediate needs have to be satisfied, and self-respect prevents them from demanding money from parents and others. Social customs and a false dignity of status prevent them from taking to manual labour or any other profession for that matter. Realization of self and the sense of responsibility have opened their eyes. This has resulted in making them careful before they fall an easy prey to the miseries of the world. Those who are brought up in well-to-do families are all the more anxious to keep up the same standard of life. An opening in life is to be made. They must be in a position to start a family independently before they get married. But how? Their efforts in getting government jobs have failed, and even if they were successful in some cases, the income realized is not enough to manage a separate house. These conditions compel them to demand a dowry to enable them to facilitate their future expenses and to try their luck in matrimonial alliances. Is it a sin that they should demand a dowry? Does it mean that they do not possess character? Does it mean that they sell themselves for money and get themselves married to unsuitable girls? Should we condemn them only because they do not live in the present?

In view of the above circumstances, what should the parents do? Should they fish for sons-in-law who demand fewer dowries or no dowry? Should they try to get their girls married to any person, irrespective of his age, character, and qualifications, only because he does not demand a dowry? If the parents, instead of wasting money on useless things, instead of squandering it on items meant for show and fame, spend it on useful things required for running a family, they will be serving two purposes. They will cooperate with the young man in his ideals and will try to make the life of the girl comfortable and happy. If a man holding a good position demands a dowry, let them not care for him who's God is wealth.

Parents should not think that the goal of a girl's life is only marriage. This idea makes them hurry over the matter. Their agitation in getting a son-in-law decreases the value of the girl. When the other party comes to know that the parents are anxious to get her married, they demand a heavy dowry. This is the way of the world. If a customer knows that the shopkeeper is anxious to sell a certain article he offers a lower price. If a seller knows the customer is anxious to buy it, he demands more money than he expected to get. Talk of marriage at home, by every member of the house from childhood, prevents the mental development of girls and accelerates the awareness of sex. The rapid growth of sex awareness results in its rapid decay. There is no stage of girlhood in the majority of cases in Indians due to a jump from childhood to womanhood. Let parents make up their minds to educate their girls and make them efficient before they get married. Let them instil a sense of independence and courage as a sense of dependence on someone for one's food and lodging, when one is forced to face the misfortunes of the world, is most deadly. The indifference of the parents towards marriage will not only increase the value of the girls but will also put a stop to the dowry system. Efficient girls will not only be an asset to the regeneration of our nation but also will be suitable companions to their educated husbands and educated mothers of their children. No girls with good education will stoop to silly customs and be left helpless in adverse circumstances. No duty is greater than making one's own children independent and making them stand on their own feet to face the misfortunes of the world.

17

The Effect of Early Marriage on Indians

Marriage occupies an important place in the life of Indians. It is a religious duty to marry and early marriage is enjoined by the Hindu code. It is the only career and the goal of life of our girls. People are of the opinion that a woman's natural life is that of wife and mother. In certain sections of the Hindu community, it is considered a disgrace for a girl to reach the age of puberty without being betrothed. Parents will go to almost any expense and trouble to prevent such a calamity. Every Hindu father longs for a son who can perform the funeral ceremonies at his death. Early marriage is indiscriminately imitated by all Indians. Even Muslims are not free of this crime. They have their own reasons for it, concocted by old grandmothers and mothers-in-law, which are mechanically hailed by men. In general, a sort of unreasonable distrust prevails among the families on both sides. Nothing is considered safe and settled until the marriage takes place. A strange belief prevails everywhere that the first offer should never be refused. A unique opportunity of securing a suitable young man comes only once in a girl's lifetime.

Suitability of young men is gauged by their economic conditions or their position in life. Often, a rich widower of sixty with innumerable children is considered a suitable husband for a girl of thirteen or fourteen. One is entitled to say that wealth is a passport to get a girl of any age in any family. There is no such idea behind the marriage 'that money is not everything'. There are other factors in one's life that are more conducive to happiness than wealth. Religious and social conditions are such that the happiness of women does not count for much. She is bound to be happy under any circumstances. Manu, the greatest Hindu lawgiver, who seems to have been very favourably disposed towards the members of his own sex has tersely decreed that 'she shall serve him (her husband) with all her might, obey him in all things, spy no defect in his character nor give him any cause of disquiet.' Marriage is meant to serve the needs of society and to propagate the nation; the maintenance of it is in the hands of God as 'when the goods increased, they are increased that eat them'.

Manu's greatest sense of partiality is evident in the rule put forward in connection with the question of divorce. He goes to the extent of advocating that a wife would not be freed from her marital ties even if her husband were to abandon her or refuse to see her. Laws are made by men and are religiously carried out by them so as not to cause any inconvenience to themselves. Do they ever think that their loose morals and other vices will create misery at home and make home life unhappy? Do they imagine that love, which is the greatest source of happiness, will not last between men and women on account of such high handedness on their part? Do they ever think that women also possess the same feelings and instincts as they do? The instinct of jealousy in a woman is as strong as in a man, though the power of its expression may differ. It is so strong in a man as to reach the pitch of committing murder. The daily newspapers bear testimony to this fact, where the initiative is always by a man. Why is this? Is it because a woman, being bodily weak, cannot attempt such a drastic punishment towards her man? The answer is simply 'no'. When, once the feeling of jealousy is created in her, she feels enough spirit to do anything beyond her physical strength but, being a puppet in her husband's hands, submits to him slavishly against her will. She is also a great advocator of the conviction that 'a good wife is one who is submissive to her husband and shows him every consideration and regard'.

The saddest of women's handicaps, however, is that of enforced widowhood. This is also sanctioned and upheld by Hindu custom, and is especially prevalent among the high castes. The most deplorable feature in the high caste Hindu community is that the widow is supposed to have been the cause of her husband's death—possibly because of sins in her previous existence. Because of this, her jewels and pretty clothes are often taken away from her. Her head is shaved. She is debarred from certain religious ceremonies. She is expected to fast to show her penitence. She is sometimes made the drudge of the household. Society objects to widow marriages even in other communities where it is not a religious dictum. Man can easily be polygamous whereas a woman cannot marry even when she is a widow. There are no such hard and fast laws for him as of breaking the marital ties. He, with all his fancies, is the noblest being ever born among the creations of God.

Marriage is a great social event in the home and country and involves many guests, many gifts, extensive feasting, music, and dancing. There are gifts of money to be made to relatives, to the witness, and to the one performing the ceremonies. The cost of feasting varies from a single meal for the guests to two or even more days of entertainment depending upon the social status and wealth of those concerned. The bride's jewellery and clothes must be bought. One half to one third of the expense of a wedding is due to the purchase of these. These must be very costly for if one is not lavish in a wedding it is taken to indicate poverty and debt. With such a reputation, it is difficult to secure good husbands for other daughters, or daughters-in-law for sons. Money must generally be paid out to secure a bride. The price paid for a bride depends upon the wealth of the bridegroom, upon his age, and upon his qualifications. Hence, it is common practice to spend from two years' to three years' income on a marriage, even in a poor family. Since the parents of a girl are obliged to undergo a great deal of difficulties in securing a husband and paying a large dowry to her prospective husband's people, baby girls are not as welcome as boys.

Malthus says, 'If it were the general custom to follow the first impulse of nature and marry at the age of puberty, virtue in the greatest conceivable degree would fail in rescuing society from the most wretched and desperate state of want.' The root cause of India's poverty could not be better expressed, for it has been the custom to follow the first impulse of nature and—fit or unfit—to marry as near the age of puberty as possible. The great curse of our country is poverty and indebtedness. It is not confined to any particular group or community. In the prosperous sections, while the necessity for borrowing is not so great, the opportunity is greater and the temptations to extravagance are often present. Hence even in the prosperous sections, money is borrowed for marriages and other social ceremonies or properties sold for the purpose.

The disadvantages of early marriages are not only economic but also include the undermining of the child mother's health, the birth of weak and sickly children, the increasing danger of overpopulation, the inadequate opportunity for wholesome food, the limited time for education before marriage, and the difficulty of educating a large number of children in later years. Another handicap grows out of the prevailing custom of Muslim women being kept secluded. The custom of a whole family crowding in a small house with little or no ventilation, lack of fresh air and sunlight has been the chief cause of high death rates among women due to tuberculosis, which is called a 'bedroom' disease. 'It runs not in the bones but in the blankets'. It spreads in, and by dark, dirty housing conditions.

The child mortality of our country needs no description. It is a well-known fact that out of ten children born, only five survive. Why is this? Are not the hospitals and the timely help given by the government and social workers enough to prevent the high death rate of infants? The answer is simple. The doctors and nurses cannot possibly take the place of a mother. They often come too late. Can we expect better results in a country where ninety per cent of our girls are married at the age of eleven or twelve and become mothers in their teens? They are expected to learn by experience. Hence, experiments are made on the first and second born. The health of the little ones depends upon the mother's efficient care and upon creating systematic and healthy habits in them. When young students leave school, they are unfit to face the great responsibility of motherhood. Mothercraft is an art; it should be taught as any other art. The teaching should be as practical as possible, with life-sized model baby dolls but not with living babies. A girl, before she enters her new life of motherhood, must be able to make a healthy and happy home and be able to face the great responsibility of 'training the character, inspiring a child with fine ideals, developing her mind, and laying the sound foundation of a healthy body'.

Early marriage comes in the way of educating our girls. There is, surprisingly, a great drop between those who start education in primary school and those who join high school. The percentage of those who enrol on a university course is not even one per cent. The difficulty of educating a large number of children can be better understood by those who undergo this penance. When the question of finance arises, the education of girls is economized on. Education of girls in backward communities is still considered superficial. Parents have not yet realized the fact that the education of a girl is more important than her marriage. Education means: to make her independent and to develop all her faculties and experience, to enable her later on to shoulder the responsibility of married life pleasantly and successfully. Whereas early marriage means: to make her a slave depending upon somebody's whims and fancies for her happiness in life and maintenance. While bringing up our girls, the attitude of parents is that the world is not a battlefield where individual effort counts for much, but a comfortable palace where there is no sunset.

Little knowledge of anything is dangerous, and a deep study is dangerous too. The former makes a person optimistic whereas the latter makes one pessimistic. Conditions at present are not so disappointing. The great thinkers and social reformers are doing much to alleviate suffering. Lala Rajpat Rai, in the course of his presidential address at the Hindu Mahasabha, Calcutta, said,

> I have the greatest admiration for the Hindu woman. She stands unique in the world in the matter of her selflessness, in her devotion to her male relations, and in her purity and chastity. But the condition of Hindu women at the present moment is far from satisfactory and that is due to the arrogance of Hindu men and to their failure of duty towards their women.

He added,

> I will beg my countrymen to save their girls, to give them suitable opportunities for developing healthy bodies and psychologically fit minds. Our girls and women must be freed from all superstition, which breeds carelessness in life, indifference to food, distaste for struggle, lack of energy, the habit of taking things lying down, and a psychology of dependence and fear.

The social reformers have established progressive societies which make arrangements for the remarriage of widows. This is done, however, in defiance of religion and custom and with the possible consequence of social ostracism. They have endeavoured hard, for many years, to raise the age of 'consent', and to educate the public regarding the dangers of early marriages. But, still, we find that hundreds of girls are taken away from schools on the pretext of marriage and are married before the age of puberty. People migrate from the place where legislation against early marriage exists to a place where it is not, in order to get their girls married. The Sarada Act is not only defeating its purpose but also creating a spirit of cheating in the people. A mere passing of laws is no good. It should be carried out strictly and systematically. Committees should be appointed and voluntary workers should come forward to prevent the masses from such an attempt. At different centres in a country, parents should be taught the dangers of early marriages; the distribution of leaflets would also help. Committees to prevent people from being extravagant in marriages would be helpful to mitigate the suffering in poorer classes. In addition to the legal punishment of parents, the law should also punish the person who marries a young girl of twelve or thirteen. An old man should never be allowed to marry a young girl. This would help to decrease the number of young widows. Experience has shown that early marriages are favoured more in the poor classes where the maintenance of a girl seems more expensive than her marriage. In coolie classes, the mother, being a working woman, tries to get rid of her responsibility of care as early as possible. For such people, vocational training for subsequent wage-earning like basket making, tailoring, bookbinding, cookery, baking, dressmaking, and laundry would improve their financial conditions. Useful education, and vocational and professional training, would be helpful in making people understand the disadvantages of early marriage.

18

The Importance of the Mother Tongue

Inaugural address delivered at the Urdu-Persian Literary Association, the Maharaja's College, Mysore, under the Chairmanship of M. A. Shustery Esq. Professor of Persian at the College

To a person his mother tongue is a 'blessing in disguise'. It is not merely a time-table subject in his education but is forced upon him from all sides. It is learnt by both the direct, or conscious, and the indirect, or unconscious, methods. The direct method supplements and regulates the knowledge gained by hearing. The mother tongue is an indispensable instrument for the development of the intellectual, moral, and physical aspects of education. It is a subject through and by which other subjects can be tackled, understood, and communicated. Clarity of thought and expression are only possible when one has a certain command over the mother tongue. Weakness in any other subject means weakness in that particular subject only, but weakness in the mother tongue means the paralysis of all thought and the power of expression. Deep insight, fresh discoveries, appreciation, and expansion of ideas are only possible when one understands the subject through being able to assimilate and be stimulated by the ideas of the subject.

The mother tongue is a factor for unification and sympathy. It unites people with a common culture, common traditions, and ideals. The common bond becomes so strong that any division is almost impossible. The sufferings of some members of the same community who speak the same language make all the rest sad, while the success of some elates the whole. This attitude of mind towards the members of one's own community is unconscious. Even the suppression of this feeling in the interests of all human beings is possible only by thinking beings. Unfortunately, the number of such widely sympathetic human beings is all too few.

The influence of the home on one's mother tongue begins during infancy. The home is the place where love and sympathy reign supreme and where they are the means of instruction. It is a place where freedom of thought and action are encouraged and practised, both by direct and indirect methods. Throughout the day, instruction in speech is given. Indistinct, unconnected utterances are checked, corrected, and transformed into clarity of expression. The child's ability to talk or make statements is developed by conversations with the parents; thus, the child's natural shyness and fear of committing mistakes are overcome. The natural gift of expression is developed.

This home influence plays a very important part in inculcating and enlarging the ideas of the child. These ideas are gathered through pictures, photographs, from articles, and by all things in the child's home and surroundings. The child's curiosity compels him to ask questions and gather information concerning everything. Enquiries about their names and uses follow. This unending stream of questions on a multitude of topics, and the degree of sensible replies or explanations given to him by his parents increases his ideas and vocabulary and, likewise, his thoughts begin to settle and his power of listening intelligently and understanding the spoken word develops.

Folk and fairy tales, and the adventures of heroes and heroines told by mothers and grandmothers have a unique value. Related in a homely manner, their chief ideas are easily understood. Such tales not only develop the character of the little one, but also improve his power of recounting what is heard. Very often, one finds little children acting out such stories. Religious instruction given at home is another aid to progress in the mother tongue. Women are usually more religious minded than men. They remember the words and music of hymns and songs. At a very young age, the child learns these by heart and later recites them before the members and friends of the family. And, sometimes, the child is bold enough to repeat them before strangers. Religious hymns and songs make an appeal to his religious instincts, which are sometimes also expressed through the medium of dolls that are made into idols. All this early learning lays a good foundation for the development of the mother tongue.

In illiterate families the influence of the mother tongue may not be so effective in the improvement of vocabulary, pronunciation, and the enlargement of ideas, but there is no lack of clear expression of some sort.

When the child enters school, he is quite familiar with words, expressions, and their uses in his daily life. Words and ideas do not seem dry and lifeless to him, as they are often used in his life. The teacher of the mother tongue is not vague in his expressions and in the presentation of facts. The homely presentation of ideas with a definite purpose creates a spirit of reciprocity in children. There is often a mutual understanding between the children and the teacher, and an appreciation of the matter read is expressed. The instinct of curiosity to know about things is satisfied by reading books written in one's mother tongue. The substance is restated in the children's own words and is turned over in their minds till they understand its meaning well. The strong foundation laid at home, and the familiarity of the ideas, make the student better fitted to cope with difficulties in school. The school supplements and regulates the knowledge gained by indirect ways. No stage of expression remains unrealized and untranslated in the pupil's life. In addition, the lectures delivered by individual speakers, debates held, and the writing of essays help to clarify the descriptions and explanations of any fresh knowledge gathered by them. The minds of children are thus prepared and ready to enter upon more advanced stages in their educational careers.

The Urdu and Persian languages, after the downfall of the Mughal Empire, did not receive due importance. They were made second languages in the syllabi of the schools, and so their position was made secondary. They were not financially supported and, hence, people neglected them because they had no market value. The country is now on the threshold of building her educational structure on the recognition of the mother tongue. It is considered an indispensable instrument for preserving one's national culture and traditions. The feeling of unrest, due to the clash between the old and new cultures, is disappearing. The Great War opened the eyes of the people and made them realize the importance of their own culture in building their nation. They agitated and adopted a uniform scheme of education. The cry of the day is to serve the nation, to develop one's own power of expression, and to preserve one's own culture and traditions. The social, political, and economic conditions of the country also accelerated the demand for a democratic form of education as a preparation for life. Consequently, the mother tongue became the rule for middle and high schools and there is an attempt to have the same in colleges and higher educational organizations.

Literary associations were started all over India, in high schools and colleges, with a view to encouraging students to actively take part in them and to create an interest in their mother tongue. Such associations have been serving a twofold purpose. They develop the students' intellect and character. They are also a means for students to do social and national service. The members solve many modern problems of life. The Literary Association of the Maharaja's College of Mysore is a wonderful living example. The activities of this association are too many to describe in detail. The very fact of inviting me from Bangalore to deliver an inaugural address is proof of the interest taken by its members in their association. The moving spirit behind it is Mr M. A. Shushtery, Professor of Persian at the college. From the time he joined the Mysore government service, a new life has entered into the students of Persian. The learning of Persian is no more a boring subject. His selfless work in the interest of his students, and in making Persian an important subject in the state, has endeared him to all those who know him and who have the good fortune of being his students. Now, people have realized the fact that the flag of the Urdu and Persian languages need not be lowered before that of other languages. The Muslims of Mysore are highly grateful to him and will always remember and cherish his memory. It is my earnest wish that the high standard of Persian raised by him will be maintained even after his retirement from state service.

19

Polygamous Marriages

In the past, polygamous marriage was considered indispensable and the only solution to solve the problem of womanhood. It was meant to protect women from the evils of society and human catastrophe, and to give them shelter and a respectful livelihood. When there was no education among them, illiteracy, ignorance, and superstition had made them puppets in the hands of man. They were unfit to stand on their own feet and to look after themselves if they were left unprotected. They lacked the power of judgement and of discrimination. They were happy with their lot of being treated as part and parcel of man's property. They had no aims and objects in life. They existed with a man's existence. If one source of help was snatched away, they were compelled to look for another. Their sufferings became worse when the male population was destroyed during wars and strife and they were left with numerous children to rear and train. Hence, the solution left for any reformer was to introduce plurality of marriage and to group them all under some protector who could look after them and save them from a life of disgrace and disrespect.

The present condition of the world is quite different from that of the past. The world is changing rapidly with its constantly changing environment. Old customs, old stimuli, and old methods of meeting them seem useless. People invent and adapt themselves to new alignments suitable to their surroundings. Old ideas are giving way to new ones. Modern education, which embodies the spirit of independence, has been the chief cause of change and progress. It has developed the intellect of society. People are in a position to judge, discriminate, and learn for themselves what is good for them. One finds that there is a desire for power, knowledge, and leadership. The contentment, which in the past was found in being ruled, is seen no more. The spirit of slavery is condemned, and that of independence and freedom is encouraged from childhood. The realization of self, and its comparison with the progress and achievements of others is the predominant factor of the day. People have begun to think collectively. A sincere regard for the progress of others, or for their achievements, is kept steadily in view by everyone. The thought of the unity and progress of a strong nation is welcomed. Individuality is found among them which make it impossible to bear the burden of others. The result is a severe fight for one's individual rights and equality. Independence, self-government, or Swaraj are the call of the day.

If this is the condition of a man, what about that of a woman? She is living in the same world as he. The rapid changes in him are to be reflected in her. The intellectual, physical, social, and political changes have altered him completely and have made him a modern gentleman. She, being his prototype, is an imitator of her intellectual lord.

If he thinks that freedom from the autocratic rulers is good for him, she thinks that freedom from an autocratic husband with unlimited powers is good for her. If he fights for his rights in the political and economic fields, she fights for her rights and against the injustices shown to her. She studies the laws and codes and criticises the intentions of the lawmakers. She pleads for justice. So, one finds the various changes in the life of man have effected a change in that of woman. She is no more a mere puppet.

Women, by nature, are not active. They are the great supporters of customs and conventions. But, one cannot say that all of them are so. There are among them some brave and observant beings, who saw the sufferings of their sisters and determined to revolt against conventions and foolish customs. They faced the social objections boldly and struggled hard against odds and adverse circumstances and paved the ground for others. Their achievement in life, and their philanthropic work in the interest of the less fortunate ones, has been a living example and an impetus to follow in their footsteps. They believe that education is the only thing that will solve the problem of womanhood. They believe that a woman with a good and useful education will not descend to slavery and foolish customs. She will be able to stand on her own feet in the adverse circumstances of the world.

'A woman's education means a nation's education' is the cry heard everywhere. Hence, there is a burning desire for getting young girls educated. No stone is left unturned to see girls educated and efficient so that they can work and

live an independent life, if need be. Marriage was the only
goal of a girl's life in the early days. Now, one finds the
goal of her life is education. Many unhappy marriages, and
the sufferings of young girls, have changed the ideas of
both the parents and the girls about marriage. Many girls
express their dislike openly and say that they will not get
married till they have graduated. The implicit resignation
to fate and complete obedience to the parents' choices
are dying out. They criticise cruelly and vehemently, the
indiscriminate actions of the parents. They believe they
can think, act, and judge in the same way as men do.
The living and thrilling example of the women of Turkey
has been an asset and an incentive in the progressive
conditions of women of our country.

Thanks must be given to the noble help offered by the
governments of our land. They have come to the rescue
of womanhood. Separate schools have been established
for them. Special facilities have been provided to them.
There are aided schools established for the same purpose.
There are private schools run by philanthropic workers
of the country. Industrial schools are open for them. The
numerous ladies' associations established for the purpose of
the upliftment of womanhood have been doing wonderful
work. There are different departments open for them in
which to work. The educational department needs their
services for the nursery and the primary stages of teaching.
Young girls have better prospects and a better future.
They need not be just one of several wives. Polygamous
marriages in such circumstances seem unnecessary. There

is no need of a larger population. The country is already overcrowded with the lean, sickly, haggard, naked, and the deformed. In our country, the number of women is not as great as it is in other countries where monogamy is the rule. If some women were left unmarried, should monogamy become a law, here they can easily take to any service. The social world needs the services of women, and as is true of the educational world. Artistic and creative activities are conducive to subordinate the sexual instinct. Intellect, being more powerful and the dominating factor in human instincts, creates individuality, self-respect, and self-regard. A monogamous form of marriage will automatically solve the educational, social, and economic problems of our country. Intellectual development has brought a decline in the world of polygamy. The notorious harems of ancient India are no longer found anywhere, the new ones have a very limited number of women. These conditions indicate that the world is ready for monogamy and the time is ripe for reformers to avail themselves of the opportunity.

20

Educated Girls in Uncivilized Families

Modern education is aimed not only at teaching girls mere facts and skills, but also at the development of their character and personality. They are made to study world opinions, ideals, and to follow the direction in which world affairs are moving. Facilities have been provided to develop the spirit of independence. They are encouraged to take an active part in the political, social, and economic activities of the country. They have big opportunities for creative thought and endeavour, which have helped them to develop their experiences. Experiments have been conducted by them in their daily lives. Their mentality is widened, their vision broadened, and their outlook on life changed. Superstition, fatalism, and the slavery of old customs have given place to realism, sensibility, and usefulness. Their ideas and ideals in growing richer and higher have meant constant adjustment of their behaviour and the development of their physical, mental, social, and aesthetic values. Their powers of judgement and criticism are mature. They have a true sense of different aspects of human life. Modern education being 'godless', their knowledge and sense of religion is almost dying out. Science has taught them to be accurate and reasonable.

What is the condition of the homes they live in and those of their mothers-in-law? The majority of the women members of the homes are illiterate, ignorant, superstitious, unscrupulous, and selfish mischief-mongers. They are more interested in the destruction of someone's life than in giving assistance to the building of life. They are elated at anyone's sufferings. In short, one may call them she-dragons (these devilish qualities may differ in some, as human nature differs). Education has no value to them. Civilization is scorned by them. The old customs and habits are so strictly followed and deep rooted that change in them is impossible. False religious principles permeate their lives, interests, and activities. Their daily activities are intimately connected with religion. Many ceremonies are performed with real devotion and religious feelings. This strong religious sense and devotion, the firm belief in a spiritual world, and the influence of ancient traditions, combine to form an atmosphere in the home which is of great importance to the inmates. Large religious gatherings, which carry out the many religious feasts, as well as pilgrimages to sacred places, have a great attraction. They will undergo any amount of hardship. They will borrow money and sell their property in order to perform the so-called ceremonies— social gatherings of ladies on some pretext or other, these providing for them wonderful opportunities for scandal and sarcastic talk.

Housekeeping is less important than food and clothing in the uncivilized circles. There is little of the artistic touch about their houses. There are usually few windows and doors. These are considered as dangerous owing to the possibility of catching cold and the fear of thieves. The persons who have the costliest jewels and clothes are respected and admired most in their group. Hence, the ambition of such ladies is to collect as many jewels and clothes as possible. In sanitation and hygiene, the condition of such a house is to be seen in the lack of drainage, in spitting in the courtyard and even in the house, the bodily waste of children, and the indifference to fleas and rats. Ignorance of the laws of hygienic living has made them an easy prey to infectious diseases. The lack of care of the infected patients has resulted in untold calamities in the family. They do not believe in the infectious nature of disease. This is due to their fatalistic philosophy, that if people are to be ill, they will be ill any way that people are fated to suffer due to the sins committed in a previous life, and so it must all be borne patiently and no attempt should be made to escape from it. Modern education teaches the girls quite different ideas and ideals about health and housekeeping. The care of the house, dress, food, and cleanliness is taught as an art, both by theory and practice. The adornment of a house and its excellence is the talk of civilized society. Girls are taught the hygienic way of living. They read the pamphlets and magazines published by the state health department.

They know the symptoms of a disease and how to prevent it from becoming serious and dangerous.

The purdah system in uncivilized circles is taken as a mark of social distinction as it necessarily makes a woman virtuous. But the purdah system observed in our country is an artificial one. It is just an external force which compels an individual to live a secluded life. It, by no means, has any effect on the human instincts. So long as the external influences are present, the instincts are suppressed but it does not mean that they are destroyed or sublimated. The minute the external force is relaxed, they demand an outlet and have their revengeful satisfaction, irrespective of self-regard and respect. Virtue is an outcome of the developed instinct of self-respect. Self-respect is the result of the sublimation of human emotion into higher and nobler motives. Virtue cannot be forced upon a person by external measures. It is an acquired object and it is acquired in one's daily life in contact with others. Hence, the purdah system observed by uncivilized women has not made them at all virtuous. This artificial purdah is neither possible nor supported by modern girls. Modern education aims at the real purdah, the development of character, personality, and the discipline of one's emotions and instincts. One can imagine the sad plight of modern girls in the family that observes artificial purdah strictly and indiscriminately, to the ruination of their health, education, and personality.

The general position and influence of women in the home is not simple or easy to describe. Motherhood is greatly venerated. The mother in a home is supreme and her word is a law which has no alternative. It must be obeyed by others at any cost. In spite of her illiteracy and ignorance, she exerts a dominating influence in the home not only over her daughters and daughters-in-law, but also over her educated sons, who look upon her with gratitude for her cultural influence. She is a religious preceptor and a teacher of ancient culture and tradition. Her love for the members of the family is often blind and indiscriminate. Her autocratic power over the members of the family has made them mere puppets in her hands. Their progress and happiness in life has to depend upon her authoritative command and her own method of dominating control—which are antagonistic to the modern age and to the sentiments of modern people. The word freedom has no meaning to her. It is beyond her power of understanding that human nature demands freedom, and that freedom of expression and action lead to progress. Each family has its own peculiar habits regarding cleanliness, adornment, method of living, of eating, social customs, and taboos. She is there to see that the members follow them faithfully, mechanically, and in exactly the same way as her grandmother and great grandmother had performed them. Any change in them means a loss of dignity for the family.

Our modern age differs from the past in every respect and aspect of human life. The cry of the day is for the appreciation of humanity as a family and for the emancipation of womanhood. Recognition of the worth of each woman in a family and her ability to put herself in man's position, both intellectually and physically, has been the aim of all social reformers. The idea of marriage as a religious duty is gradually dying away. The wife in the modern world is accepted as a companion and a participant in every aspect of her husband's life. She is expected to help him in his intellectual, political, social, and economic activities. She is the maker of a sweet home for him and also an educator of his children—but not an economic necessity to replace a servant. Educated ladies all over India have started many well-organized associations to create goodwill and cooperation among the members of their sex. They have tried to prevent the contemptuous attitude of superiority and inferiority which is supposed to be the mark of social distinction. There is the realization of self in contact and interaction with other selves. Modern education has made girls revolt against old customs which are barriers to their progress. Naturally their intellectual, social, and moral contact with the uncivilized and illiterate women at home causes friction and misunderstanding. An educated member in an uneducated family is an obstacle to the happiness of the rest. She is expected either to change her habits and ideas and adjust herself to the surroundings or make her life miserable. Habits formed from childhood become second nature and are unchangeable, so these produce more causes for friction and bitterness.

Educated mothers and girls, too, should not be led away by sentimentalism, glamour, and the enviable position of men in life. They should think of the cruel, illiterate, and ignorant women of the house with whom the girl has to live. The happiness of the girl is more important than her being called the member of a rich and well-known family. Wealth and fame are not conducive to happiness. It is the ideas, ideals, temperaments, and outlook on life which are the sources of comfort and happiness. The joint family system, which was a blessing in the dark ages when all the members were sailing in the same boat, has now become a curse. The microscopic educated minority, in the hands of the overwhelming illiterate majority is either tortured or is doomed to ruin.

21

HH The Maharaja of Mysore*

His Highness, the most benevolent, truly a great
and lovable personality, loves the land he rules
and lives for it. He loves liberty, equality, and
cooperation. His every word, thought, and deed expresses
this feeling. His clear and deep thinking and his impartial
treatment of his subjects have been the chief causes of the
progress and prosperity of the country. His treatment of
women is quite modern. He gives them equal liberty and
education with men.

Freedom of humanity is the watchword of his rule.
Attempts have been made to give freedom to people in
all aspects of life—educational, social, and political. The
spirit of independence is inculcated and instilled from the
school-going age. In almost all the schools and colleges,
attempts have been made to give the true and right sort of
education by developing the faculties of the mind. Physical
development is attempted with the help of sports, games,
physical culture, swimming, riding, etc. In addition various
means and methods are sought for, and used, to achieve
this end. Students are sent to the most advanced countries

*His Highness died while this book was at the press.

of the world, where the spirit of independence reigns supreme. Students studying at high schools and colleges are encouraged to run various associations, unions, and societies. The senior students are made responsible for their satisfactory working. There are dramatic and literary associations, and debating societies coupled with as many societies as there are subjects. The students invite eloquent speakers and well-known men of letters, and arrange for their lectures and entertainments. They are free to hold discussions on the most controversial subjects of the day. Such activities are encouraged not only by the teachers and professors but also by others who are independent-minded and know the intentions of their ruler. This complete freedom of expression and action has fostered their individuality, has given them an idea of self and of their ability. It has also helped to build their personalities and morality. This is the true and the only education according to nature.

The treatment of teachers in the state also needs mention. In addition to training colleges and schools, much more has been attempted to increase their efficiency and individuality. Different vocational and physical courses and classes are arranged during the holidays and teachers are forced to attend them. These help to rekindle their enthusiasm and to develop their spirit of adventure. Teachers cannot indefinitely be giving of their best without replenishing their own stores. No teacher can, in his or her own grade, be too highly gifted or too highly trained. The teacher is the lever, so his ability inevitably raises the spirit of the young ones entrusted to his charge. A panel of men and women who are recognized authorities on their own subjects are engaged to deliver lectures upon educational, religious, and social topics in schools and colleges. These lectures have the important social effect of counteracting wrong influences and are conducive to harmony.

One of the chief objectives of His Highness is to raise the quality and level of culture among his subjects, and especially among the masses. The demand for freedom is an outcome of a developed culture and self-realization. With this aim in view, he encourages everyone, of every community, by providing them with opportunities to be educated. Different kinds of vocational and night schools have been established for all. Much attention has been paid to both their extension and their quality. Things that are really important to them are taught. To make their education real and useful, various measures are used and educational appliances have been provided.

His subjects have been given freedom of association, movement, and expression. They may go wherever they like and settle down. They are not prevented from travelling to any place to earn their living. No sort of restriction is placed on the free movement and action of even strangers. The people have been given the right of association and the right to form social, religious, or political societies where they think, consult, and discuss together about matters of common interest. They have the power to express their opinions in their meetings. The freedoms of press and platform have been powerful organs for educating the public. Thus, the policy and action of the government has been based, to a great extent on public opinion. The only restriction put on them is that they should not abuse their powers by defaming other persons or bringing the government into contempt. Honest criticism and suggestions are welcomed, so that any existing wrongs may be remedied. These meetings and speeches, and consequent actions have resulted not only in benefit to the people but also in the improvement of the government itself. They have been the basis of the demand for responsible government. These associations are not declared unlawful except for very strong and necessary reasons.

His Highness is the signpost of religion, but he has great religious tolerance. He has as much respect for another's faith as he has for his own. People are free to worship as they like and to entertain any religious belief. He never compels them to follow any particular religion or to believe in a certain doctrine. Moral and religious instruction form the essential part of a pupil's education in all schools. High ideals and deeper feelings are instilled in them from a very early stage of education. His tolerance of religious principles has helped people cooperate and work together in all cultural and useful affairs of the state. It has also helped to nip the great curse of communal feelings in the bud. The maintenance of a peaceful environment has been the chief cause of the rapid progress of the country.

His Highness patronizes the Scout movement. It creates opportunities for the full development of the spirit of adventure and independence. It helps to develop a sound mind in a sound body. It helps to cultivate the habits of observation, right thinking, and correct judgement. It encourages the youth to learn by doing. It helps to make them useful, purposeful, patriotic, young citizens of the country. It gives them freedom of thought, expression, and action in the service of others. Even the rural uplift scheme of our state aims at starting Cub packs and Scout troops in the villages for the benefit of the masses.

One is entitled to say that the attitude of the ruler towards the Harijans is very partial (it ought to be for a time). He takes special interest in their education, social, and political progress. Special schools have been established for them, in addition to freedom given for admission in all other schools and colleges. Special opportunities have been provided for their education, with particular attention to their needs and circumstances. Scholarships, free ships, and exemptions from examination fees are generously sanctioned. Free distribution of clothes, slates, and books is made both in special and general schools for them. They enjoy the freedom of special hostels with free boarding and lodging.

In order to improve their financial condition, special concessions, by way of free lands, loans without interest, free grants of timber and bamboo for building sanitary houses, and also agricultural implements have been sanctioned and provided generously. Arrangements have been made to teach them thrift and to develop the spirit of cooperation among them. A large number of cooperative societies have been established for the Harijans.

They are allowed representation in all the great constitutional bodies of the state. Special representation, through nomination in political associations, is made. In government services, qualified candidates of this class are given preference over those of other communities. All public places are opened to them without distinction of caste, creed, or colour. To instil courage, hope, and self-reliance into them, special measures have been sought for and tried. Thus the ideas of inequality in constitutions of society and that of untouchability are dying out of our country. What Mahatma Gandhi has been doing for Harijans is not a matter of great wonder to us when we think of what our noble ruler has been doing for them in the whole state.

Attempts have been made, with great success, to relieve the masses from financial worries. Industrial training, partly for the development of the country and more properly for individual development, is given. They are trained not only for the purpose of giving them a livelihood but also for a fuller life. Measures for this purpose are too many to mention. Different factories, mills, and mines are at work. Many dams are built and are under construction. Many experiments, such as the curing of tobacco, making of electric light bulbs, glass, paper mills, and so on, are also in hand and promise to be successful. Thousands of people are employed and food is supplied to the poor villagers of the state.

The construction of the beautiful public buildings, broad roads, avenues, small parks, circles, squares, fountains, floodlights, and gardens in Mysore is for a definite purpose—to beautify the city and thereby to create a beautiful environment and unite all without distinction of caste or creed. This, again, is an outcome of his idea of giving liberty to his subjects. These fine places have educational, social, physical, and aesthetic value. Thousands of people meet there daily, and exchange ideas and ideals.

The most striking proof of his love for liberty is in the constitution and in the organization of his government. He appoints different committees on constitutional reform to examine, in detail, the working of the government, and also committees for finance, medicine, public health, and a special committee to advise the government on constitutional and political questions. All these committees have administrative powers in their own spheres. The proposals and suggestions put forward by them are put into practise. Though he is the executive head of the government, the real administration is in the hands of the Executive Council. He remains supreme nominally and has given as large a share of the administration to his people as possible. The policy of the government is extended with the increasing consciousness of his subjects.

The Legislative Council associates the non-official gentlemen with the affairs of the government. It is granted a constitutional status. It has powers to make laws and to regulate them. The franchise was extended to increase their number. Members discuss the budget, move and cut motions, and vote upon the demands for grants. They have an effective voice in deciding the financial policy of the government. They can also move resolutions on matters of general and public interest.

The Representative Assembly has the privilege of placing, before the government, the wants, wishes, and grievances of the people, and the power to set them right. It expresses public opinion in matters of legislation, taxation, finance, and administration. It deals with all legislative matters before they are put before the Legislative Council. Members discuss the principles and policy of the proposed subjects and express their opinions. No taxation can be levied before their opinion is ascertained. It also has the power to move resolutions on the budget according to its principles and also on matters of public importance. It criticises government measures.

Institutions of local self-government have been established in almost every village of the state. Members have the right to elect their president, and through an elected majority. The interference of the government in their affairs is minimal. There are different kinds of boards with powers to control their own finances and manage their own local matters. They are given the power to discuss and pass resolutions on many local subjects and submit the same directly to the government. All important duties concerning the welfare of the people are entrusted to them. Local self-government is gaining great importance in extent and efficiency on account of the responsible part and position it holds and plays in the service of the people of the various places.

It is an established fact that His Highness has unceasingly devoted long years of his rule and has never spared himself from the strenuous task of taking an interest in affairs that concern the progress and prosperity of his country and his people. He has endowed India, particularly Mysore, with a rich heritage of profound wisdom. The following quotation from one of his speeches is a little example of his goodness.

My faith in the power and willingness of my people to render patriotic service is firmly rooted in experience and you may rely on my abiding sympathy with your aspirations. If every act of yours is guided by common sense, goodwill, and the useful study of facts and of experience, if your new powers are used only for the promotion of the common good, you cannot fail to rise in power and influence. You will help to build up the prosperity and reputation of our state and will become custodians with me of its permanent interest.

No nobler message could be given to his subjects by a ruler.

22

Tribute to 'The Deccan Times'

It is a matter of great honour and pleasure to us, Muslims, that the *Deccan Times* has successfully passed the most precarious period of its life—infancy. Infant mortality in our country, due to lack of care and nourishment, has produced great havoc. Many parents have been left childless, and their efforts at saving the lives of innocent beings have failed. The parents of the *Deccan Times* are experienced and their attempts in bringing up the child have been admirable. They have built up the mind and the body of the child systematically. He is strong enough, in his childhood, to travel all over India and to many other countries abroad. His mind, in the hands of his well-educated parents, has been psychologically developed. Different faculties of his mind have reached the stage of maturity. He is able to think, judge, and criticise.

Now he is entering the age of boyhood which is the most active period of life. Mental and physical activities at this age have to pave the ground for those of his future life and career. He, being well brought up from his childhood shows very promising signs of his brilliant success in serving Muslims, in particular, and Indians in general. Hence, one is entitled to say that the young boy stands before his parents, the Muslims, healthy, happy, helpful, and full of hopes and aspirations, to be known in the whole world and to reach the house of every Muslim whether rich or poor, with the motives of uniting them all for the common good, restore Muslim women to the rightful position given to them in Islam, spreading the real Islamic principles in the darkest houses and to enlighten Muslims by examples to fight for their causes and rights. Now it is the duty of the parents to understand his ideals and ambitions, to encourage him, and support him in his achievements. They will well deserve the appreciation and admiration of the world if they try to make him a guiding star for those in quest of truth, knowledge, and beauty; with a view to unite, to create goodwill and bring peace in the name of those ideals and virtues for which the Prophet lived and died.

A paper, in the modern age, is a formidable weapon in the hands of a nation. It enables the people to express their convictions, grievances, and rights with sufficient strength. It is capable of many possibilities, is ready to arm and help, and is good for offence and defence. It speaks of the concepts of the whole living Muslim community taken as a synthesis. So, it is a unifying organ. India, being in the formative stage of her political, intellectual, social, and administrative development, the progress and prosperity of such an instructive and informative organ in the interest of the nation is indispensable.

It is a pity that people in general have not realized the great value of knowledge— 'a fragment of knowledge is worth more than a hundred prayers'. It is as essential to human life as is water and air. Why don't people believe in buying knowledge as they do in purchasing other commodities of life?

If only parents would make their children buy useful things such as papers in their own name they would be doing a double service to them. The children would be proud of the paper because they pay for it, and they would be compelled to read it and gather information. This would naturally develop a spirit of sympathy and help towards their brethren. It is to be hoped that the journal will do a better service by becoming a daily paper.

This is my sincere message to the *Deccan Times*.

23

Group Psychology and India

Man, by nature, is a lover of liberty, leadership, power, and domination. He wants a field to display all these impulses. There, expression gives satisfaction and happiness. There is nothing more pleasing to a man than to see the fruits of his labour. A repeated display of these impulses, from childhood makes him crave for their fuller expression to secure, if possible, an important place in home, society, and the government of his country and, if luck has it, attain international fame. He is anxious to see that his value is recognized and his personality respected everywhere. He bends his will to achieve his object. He attempts to enter into the affairs of his country and to share the fruit of cooperative efforts, both in satisfying his own needs and in nearing his object on the plea of social service. He enriches his life by making use of all natural resources—social, cultural, and material. He delights in holding a place of responsibility in public affairs and in guiding his fellow men. Material concern is not very great in matters like this. Man is held up at every stage, and in every step of his attempt, by counteracting influences. These put hindrances and obstacles in his progress. He finds himself in a fix and does not know how to act. He begins to criticise, and find fault with antagonistic opposition and with sanctioned authority. He craves for liberty, equality, and justice. This attitude of mind does not take him far in the attainment of his ideal. He gives up his strivings in despair.

Humanity is divided into different types. There are different people suited to different purposes. There are some in whom the instincts of food-seeking, combat, self-pity, self-assertion, and a good power of expression are stronger than other instincts. Such personages occupy the position of leaders, reformers, and outstanding demi-gorgons. They are imbued with the principles of collective psychology. They successfully dominate their fellow men. They know the art of suggestion and express their ideas emotionally, inspire enthusiasm, exalt their feelings, and infuse their ideals in those who admire leaders and imitate them in every walk of life.

The food-seeking instinct is very strong in every human being. It clamours for immediate satisfaction, being the first requirement of self-preservation. It becomes keener and keener in man when he completes his educational career or passes the age of dependency and feels in a position to stand on his own feet. He strives to get an opening but is disheartened when he does not find one or if social status and other considerations prevent him from availing of the offer. Failure in his attempts does not kill his spirit; on the other hand, the instinct of combat is energised in him. He approaches the source from which he wants to get his food. He examines its organization and its working. He obtains a complete knowledge of its varying aspects and phases and finds that he has no chance of securing a place there. He then starts attacks, directly and indirectly, and begins antagonistic propaganda against it. The failure of the instinct of combat gives birth to that of self-pity. He summons help from others on the pretext of injustice, capitalism, and corruption being rampant in the government and in other bodies. His anger gives him strength and knowledge to express his ideas with feeling and emotion. He expresses them in ways to justify his actions and attitude towards the authority, so that his listeners take it all as the Gospel truth. His spirit is reinforced and his curiosity makes him interested in objects outside his goal. He takes part in other activities to know how things work and stand. He picks up information regarding his object, adds something to it, subtracts something from it, and puts his own made up concoction before his fellowmen.

A person with a developed impulse of self-assertion assumes the role of a leader. The instinct is stimulated into activity by the presence of inferior fellow beings. It encourages the possessor to display, to his audience, a mental or physical superiority in some direction or other. This expression is followed by the joy of mastery. Thus, he feels contented to plod along, asserting his powers again and again. He knows the art of suggestion as a potent factor, both for weal and woe; his tactful suggestion creates a hypnotizing effect on the minds of his listeners. Evil-minded people are the incarnation of the power of suggestion. They achieve their object with the least exertion by bringing in petty reasons, lame excuses, and unconvincing ideas to justify their actions and attitude against the object of their hatred.

The inhabitants of any country can be classified into three groups—the crowd, the club, and the community.

The crowd—the illiterate and an ignorant majority—forms an organism in which there is not much individual thought and feeling, but collective thought and feeling. Action is the characteristic of this group. It forms a dense gathering, very punctual in obeying mechanically fixed rules and principles, especially religious codes. A particular date, time, and manner have to be specified for these and they have to be done, though the heavens may fall. For instance, going to a church, a temple, a mosque has to be done without fail. No obstacle, however great and insurmountable, will prevent them from doing so. Any slackening in its working will upset them beyond measure. When such a gathering passes one will find that every one of them is bent upon his own task and cares very little for the group of which he is a member. But, if something happens on the way, their normal condition is disturbed and the eyes and attention of all is directed to the occurrence. A common interest cooperates them all and excites them equally. Very often, an emotional cry and action follows. Their mental life knows no change, but they feel, act, and think together. In normal conditions, the thinking, acting, and feeling of each individual may differ and may be of a higher level, but the mental life of the group is of a much lower level than its individual modes. Political and religious processions are the typical expressions of their mental life. In the group life, the individuality of a person is cramped and is subservient to the needs of the whole.

The gregarious instinct is very strong in the crowd. Its manifestation welds them all into passive and submissive beings. They possess a strong sense of imitation. When they see others acting, they copy instinctively. One instinctive action is followed by another. Their minds, not being disciplined, have never learnt to think. Hence, they take all that is put before them for granted. The ideas put forward by others are accepted unwittingly. This often leads them to commit blunders. They have no sentiments or memories, and even their consciousness is strictly limited. Their modes can be compared to the perceptual level of mental development which follows the impulse of the moment. They implicitly obey the dictates of their leader in spite of difficulties. The perception of instinctive behaviour in him unlocks their instincts. Real mob panic and mob anger are due to the leader's emotional enthusiasm. The club group contains a slightly more advanced type of population. One is entitled to bring the half-educated or half-intellectual section into this category. Its members have a sort of common sentiment or ideal which unites them into a collective organism. When they are together, a new force or activity is at work and their collective support brings it into action. The common ideal unifies them all because they possess the power of sharing the feelings of others. They are capable of seeing the viewpoint of others and of upholding it.

They also are imitative, but it is not mechanical or instinctive. They imitate the customs, traditions, arts, and civilization of their elders and others in every aspect of their life. Their imitation has not cramped their individuality greatly. The idea of change and progress is there but, not being systematically directed, they often go astray and imitate things indiscriminately. Things that are beyond their power of maintenance attract their minds; and this imitation causes misery and dissatisfaction. The following quotation gives a clear idea of the life and the ideal of this group. 'The most original minds discover themselves only in playing the sedulous ape to others who have gone before them along the same path of assertion.'

The community is the third group and is the, smallest. (It is not quite correct to speak of a Muslim or Hindu community as the members of it do not possess all the qualities a community needs.)

The community is held together by a comprehensive common purpose. There is a difference in each member. No two persons hold exactly the same opinions on all matters. The members not only share the feelings of others but also their thoughts. They appreciate the thoughts of writers and are absorbed in reading. They delight in the thoughts of their favourite writers because they find an analogy between their own thoughts and those of the writers.

The purpose put forward by them is a comprehensive one. It is often the result of deliberate consideration in the interests of the community, or of the people for whom they work. Each member regards the community in its different settings and accepts and takes it as his own aim in life and uses it as a field for his activities. Being strong and effective, it not only gathers them all together but focuses the whole life of its members. The community also enables them to achieve complete self-realization and a relationship between self and others. Imitation with this group is neither mechanical nor imitative but is, rather, a means to original self-expression. Nothing is completely imitated by them. An object of imitation is analysed and, after seeing its pros and cons, it may be adopted.

The innate capacity to think, judge, and act is the chief cause of their success. They possess a highly developed intellect and their organizations are run systematically with a purpose. The various associations established, both by men and women, are the symbols of their intellect. In the mind of each member, there is an idea of its nature, composition, function, and of the individual's relationship with the whole. The interaction between the members of one association with others of different ideas and ideals leads not only to cooperation but also facilitates the working out of their ideals. The united cooperative spirit creates a sincere idea of social service. A love of mankind burns in the hearts of the many.

The instincts of self-assertion in leaders, and of submission in the led, find an outlet, a field of activity, in the word 'democracy'. The life of an average being, without such an avenue of expression would be dull and uninteresting.

The word 'democracy' also promises a solution of the
social and economic problems of the country. It means
(according to them) to change the form of government and
the philosophy of life. The next quotation expresses their
motive in demanding democracy.

One of the great objects of civilization is to suppress force
and to exact the rule of reason. Therefore, as men come
under the influence of democratic ideals and spirit they
find a larger individual and community liberty and fewer
forcible restrictions are put upon their life, while the
individual is led out into a large life, which is the life of the
mind, of the soul, and of the spirit, which the trained and
healthy body is educated as the instrument to serve.

Such ideals work wonders on the masses. They are
encouraged to participate in all the essential needs of life.
They demand a right to control the means by which their
necessities are satisfied and further social status can be
raised because 'democracy is the government of all, by all, for
all, under the leadership of the wisest and the best'. Hence,
the law of the country, which is meant for the safeguarding
of life, liberty, and social welfare, is violated. The freedom
of the press, the platform, and other agencies meant for
educating public opinion is criticised and condemned.
Authority is questioned and challenged and discontent
shown against sanctioned beliefs, theories, customs, and
laws. Often attacks are made without the least consideration
for the old principles and customs. The 'divine right of
kings' and implicit submission to such authority, which is

an approved custom from time immemorial and which was sanctioned by the people themselves, cannot be transferred or shattered at once. Love of power is aspired to by human nature and every human being wants to have it. It ought to be worshipped by the man who enjoys it as a birthright. The transfer of one's own power to others is not an ordinary thing but is an expedient which entails great sacrifice and selflessness. One can learn a lesson from the present war, how the sacrifice of everything else is subordinated to that one object. Capitalism, the ill distribution of wealth, and regard for social status in a country, have been the work of many centuries, carried out by those in authority or position. Counteraction will also take several centuries to change and crush this growth.

The democracy contemplated by the people is an ideal yet to be achieved. It requires the basic education of the majority of our people. We need a good number of ideal men and women who will be able to take part in the political, social, religious, and educational activities of the country. Their characters must be developed to enable them to do their duties justly and efficiently. They should be able to suppress the social dogmas, and affect a revolution in traditions and customs. They should he more generous in understanding the values, interests, and ambitions of others. The goal of life of the people should be the growth and development of every man and woman, and not the valuation of his products. Let everyone be a leader himself, instead of depending upon others to lead him. Then alone, man will be free to achieve freedom from his own worst self, from ignorance, prejudice, and selfishness. Mere absence of restraint is not freedom. Everyone needs the wilful and purposeful social identification of his or her own self.

24

Impressions of a Visit to Europe

Countries like England, Switzerland, Turkey, and Egypt have realized the fact that any progress, if it is to be real and effective, has to be through womanhood. The destiny of a nation, to a great extent, lies in the hands of its women. No race, society, or nation can be brave, noble, and true, unless women make it so. This fact has made the people of those countries impart sound education to women as well as raise their status. Hence, every possible facility and opportunity has been provided for the purpose. The social, spiritual, moral, intellectual, and physical aspects of life have been paid attention to adequately. This kind of treatment has undoubtedly resulted in the development of their personality and character. It is apparently fallacious to say that modern Western civilization and the freedom of women have resulted in demoralising women. The women of other countries, brought up under different circumstances, would not demonstrate the right use of such liberty and social progress of women. Excepting a few details, this can undoubtedly be copied as a model of our future civilization.

Homes, schools, societies, and of churches in England, in particular, pay more attention to the development of one's character than to one's intellect, as character develops before intellect begins. No wonder then that the average English person is so noble, honest, and straightforward. The English people, in general, and the police in particular, are ever-ready to render service or help those in need, especially foreigners. Their sympathetic understanding, gentleness of manner, systematic discipline, and firm moral character are very impressive.

It is impossible to enumerate the names of all my friends and their kindnesses towards me during my stay there. But, I shall just mention a few names of important personages whose loving treatment and sincerity of friendship will be ever remembered gratefully. These are Viscountess Astor, Lady Baden-Powell, Dame Katherine Furse, and Miss G. M. Hall. Just to mention an instance of the bewitching manners of these ladies, one day at a private dinner with Miss Rathbone, the MP, I stayed until late in the night, talking busily with her. The subjects of conversation, India and Mysore in particular, being of absorbing interest, the passage of time was not noticed. It was gratifying to hear her speaking in glowing terms of the efficiency of the administration of Mysore, adding that, if other states were as good, Indian affairs would not worry them. When she asked how this state is so much better and different from the others, I had to say that it was due to the enlightened Maharaja and his Prime Minister.

I only wish that more Indians could afford to go to England and mix with such people, who may be called gems of humanity, and thus help to clear the present misunderstanding. The narrow view of events has made some people antagonistic to the West and its civilization. To encourage this tendency is to plunge the East deeper into the mire. What we ought to realize is that Western civilization is a modern one built on the experiences of many centuries in the East and the West. To turn away from it, as if it were something alien or hostile to us, is to misread the lessons of history. On the contrary, we ought to welcome in it all the seeds of progress and all the healthy elements that help to conquer or cure the ailments into which any human system may fall.

Leading modern educational thinkers in the West have influenced educational methods to a great extent. Much of what they teach has been scientifically tested and their educational systems have been greatly psychologized. My personal interest in the education of Indian women made me not only write a thesis on the above subject but also led me to visit different schools in England, Turkey, and Egypt. In these countries, more attention is paid to the practical side of education than the theory. Music, handicraft, and physical culture are made compulsory subjects. In all government schools, books are supplied to all the pupils, irrespective of their material conditions, and all other needs to help general education are provided. The government and the people have realized the real meaning of education and provide the immediate needs of the country. The spirit of the revival of national life has made them spend their money for the interest of the nation and not for privileged individuals only. The aim of education in those countries is the continuity of knowledge and a connection between the student life and the future life. Efficiency of the person is considered to be of paramount importance in the views of both the government and the people. The sheer waste of money, age, and faculties which are obviously seen in India cannot be seen in any part of the whole world. Education is meant to supply the needs of home, society, and the country and not to bring a big cleavage as is unfortunately the case in our country.

For my visit to such schools, I am indebted to the Turkish ambassador in London and to the minister of education of Egypt in London who made arrangements for me through the directors of education in Turkey and Egypt. Not only did the directors spare the valuable services of one of the female inspectors to go around with me, but also provided conveyance.

It is my sincere wish that, when the present war is over, all interested in the public life of this country will visit Europe, with a sense of impartiality and see things as they are.

25

My Experience in
an English University

An extension lecture delivered under the auspices of the Mysore University, 29 November 1935

I have been asked to speak to you tonight about 'My Experience in an English University'. I do know I am not competent to speak authoritatively on the aims and workings of English universities on the basis of my short stay in England for two years. Fortunately for me, I am asked to speak on my experiences and, if what I may say tonight does not meet with your approval, I may be kindly excused on the plea that they are my experiences. Our experiences in life are more often bitter than pleasant and I will be failing in my duty if I do not narrate all my experiences during my short stay in England.

The thought of going to an English university entered my mind immediately after I got my degree at Mysore in 1930. But, what with the disability of my sex and of leaving my six children, the youngest of whom was only five years old, often I thought it was a mad idea and an idle dream, but sometimes dreams come true. For a period of two years, it occupied my mind, increasing gradually in its complexity and force until, during the summer of 1933, it became an accomplished fact. My eldest son, who graduated from Madras University in 1933, was determined to proceed to England for higher studies and ICS training. This was a driving force for me to accomplish my own strong desire which I had cherished in my mind for over two years. It will be out of place in this lecture if I proceed to narrate the difficulties we had to encounter in the matter of arrangement for our departure. I applied to our government for the award of a scholarship to me but unfortunately it was not given and I was told that scholarships for education were not given, as if the education of our country, especially that of women, had come of age and hence it needed no further attention or encouragement. This refusal was a bombshell but the desire in me was so deep-rooted that I determined to proceed against all odds. On the tenth of September, I left Bangalore for Colombo with my son. The depressed condition of my little ones needs no description. We took a Japanese ship from Colombo that was supposed to be the cheapest of all others. It took twenty-five days to reach England. Both of us are poor sailors, but I proved to be the worst and for seventeen days I was in bed and lived only on water and fruits. We reached London on the eighth of October. I lack the words to describe the thrill of joy we felt on landing in the country which we had cherished to visit for a long time. I will be false to myself if I do not remember tonight the joy we felt when we saw Mr Rice, the trade commissioner, and his assistant, Mr Murthy, on the deck, asking people for us. Mr Rice was informed of our arrival by Mr Humayun Mirza Ismail. I was moved by their social nature and readiness to help others in need. We were taken to the High Commissioner and other people and they said that, if my son was aiming at the ICS, he must be left in London. As my financial condition could not permit me to stay in the university halls, I decided to live in private lodgings where boarding and lodging were given at a comparatively less cost. A lady was in charge of the halls for ladies, who was careful to see that no lady student coming to study in the university from outside stayed in private lodging. When she came to know that I had been granted admission to the university she wrote a letter of welcome to the Halls to me, pointing out the advantages of living with the other lady students. But I did not reply to her letter. On the other hand, I informed the secretary of the Indian Association to meet me at the station. The president of the Association also met me at the station. The president of the Association also told me that a room in one of the nearest halls to the university at Leeds has been reserved for me by Miss Hibgame, but I requested them to recommend me to some lodging. I reached Leeds at 5.30 in the evening. It was very dark and raining and I stayed for the night in a registered lodging.

Next morning, at nine o'clock, Mr Ghose, the secretary of the Indian Association, came to take me to the university. We first went to Education House to see Miss Blackburn, principal of the women's section. The secretary knocked at the door and went in to inform the authorities about my arrival. To my surprise, the principal herself came to welcome me saying that she was anxiously waiting for me.

One never finds servants sitting idly in front of doors as we see here. She herself brought a chair and made me sit down. She questioned me on various topics, ranging from the weather, convenient journey on the sea, to conditions in India. The conversation then turned to the university, the subjects taught there, and other things relating to my purpose. She also asked me about my school, the subjects I was interested in. I was then introduced to Professor Smith, the Head of the Department of Education, who happened to meet us.

It was ten o'clock and Miss Blackburn had a lecture. She asked me if I would go with her to the lecture theatre. On my agreeing to do so, she took a big attaché case containing books, pictures, and papers and asked me to accompany her. Though old, bordering on 60 years of age, she was more energetic and active than a normal Indian of half her age. We had to get down the steps and, to my surprise, before I got down two of them, she was down on the floor waiting for me. We walked to the university and had to pass long corridors. When we were still half the way to the lecture theatre, the bell had gone. She seemed excited and extended her arm, perhaps to take mine in hers. But, as I was not used to this kind of familiarity in Indian universities, I offered my notebook to her thinking that was what she wanted. She just took it, turned this way and that way, and returned it to me. Evidently, she did not want to embarrass me by saying that she did not want the book. We climbed up to the lecture theatre which was on the third floor and, before I was comfortably seated, Miss

Blackburn had already removed her coat, hat, and gloves, and was taking the attendance. How ashamed I was of my wonderful impracticability! She called my name and, as I could not understand her pronunciation, I did not answer. I thought she was calling the name of some Mrs Hoozan though I came to know afterwards that in a class of eighty students there was no other 'Mrs'! After the lecture was over, she joined me again and took me to a secluded place and asked me to pronounce my name. After I did it, she repeated it twice and told me she would not forget it. The other lecturers, too, did the same thing.

She then directed one of the students to take me to Miss Hibgame, the Secretary of the Halls. The latter welcomed me heartily and began to ask me about my lodging, saying that she had already reserved a room for me in Lyddon Hall. We decided to go to Lyddon Hall. It was another trial for me to walk with one whose steps seemed so light that they hardly touched the ground. We went to the warden, a nice old lady who, on seeing me approached me, with a smiling face and hands outstretched to welcome me. I was then taken to my room, which I must call a blue room where everything including the bed, curtains, carpet and vase with lovely blue flowers was all blue. There was a lovely fire burning and a bedstead was spread near it, so that it might be warm. My things were ordered to be brought from the lodgings and I became an inmate of the hall against my previous determination.

The dinner hour came and, as the bell was heard, a beautiful girl came to my room to take me to the common room where all the students and wardens meet and where they choose their partners for dinner. As soon as I entered the hall I saw the principal, who came to me and asked me whether I would like to be her partner. It puzzled me and I only said 'yes'. She, at once, took my arm in hers and stood majestically talking to me and to the other students of the hall. Meanwhile, I very keenly watched the other people accepting such offers. The acceptance was in the following terms—'I would love to be', or 'with great pleasure','Yes, thank you', and so on. The second gong was heard. Miss Blackburn led me first, and the rest followed us. We went to a table where the warden with her partner, and the executive members of the hostel committee also joined us. After a small prayer by the warden we sat down to dinner. All the time, my partner had an eye on me enquiring about my needs. What a contrast with the kind of airs we are accustomed to seeing in our professors here. She was trying to find out my aptitude and interests. The more shyer a girl was, the more freer she was with her, to make her shake off her shyness. After dinner, we went back to the common room in the same grand procession and had a hearty talk; as all the students began to put questions on India and social customs, etc. Then the girls danced and the warden played on the piano. My partner asked me whether I knew dancing. I have been dwelling upon these details just to impress upon you the kind of relationship that exists between students and professors in England. In all cases, the initiative of forwardness originates from the professors. How I wish the same atmosphere prevailed over here.

Every year, when the term begins, the Vice Chancellor's reception in honour of the freshers to the university is a grand function. Shortly after I entered the university, I had the pleasure of an invitation from the Vice Chancellor to this annual function. The staff is also invited. There were 3,000 students and 75 members of the staff. The Vice Chancellor and his wife received every one of us during this function and one could see professors and students playing indoor games as equals. Some teachers took it as a great pleasure to serve tea and other refreshments to students. The Vice Chancellor and his wife could be seen on this occasion, moving about and talking to every one of the invitees.

Another striking instance was the reception given to the students and staff by the public of the place. I was pleased to find that they had developed a sense of internationalism. They were posted with the most up-to-date information relating to the different countries from which students had come. The public get a list of students, with their nationality and country noted against each, from the university and invites them to tea and for the weekend. Lest the invitees should find it inconvenient to find their residences, they send them the maps and plans of their houses or sometimes personally take them to their houses. This shows the keen interest the public and the parents take in the cause of education which is so woefully absent in India. We, in

India, do not treat the members of this noblest but sorriest of professions—I mean the teaching profession—with the respect which its workers so richly deserve.

You may be interested to know something about the course of training given to students at an English university. What I am going to say is the practice at Leeds University and it is much the same in any other English university. You will see how it radically differs from the training given to students here in India. In India, intellectual work is the dominant, if not the only, factor that is kept in view. Students sit in their classes from 11 a.m. to 5 p.m. and receive all the information that is given to them by the several teachers. We are all familiar with the examination bogey. There are examinations in all countries in the world but the evil of making much of the results of examinations is peculiar to India. This is because an average Indian parent regards the education of his son or daughter as a financial investment capable of fetching a high price in the market. Education, therefore, is desired not for acquisition of culture but of gain and a good job in service. On account of this worship of results, the poor students are crammed, notes are dictated, and all possible questions are answered, so that anything important from the examination point of view is stuffed into the students and anything unimportant from that viewpoint, even though of high educational value, is rejected. The result is that there is only time for cramming and cramming alone, and absolutely no time for education and culture. You are all familiar with the statement 'A sound mind in a sound body'. Unfortunately in India the latter is given little or no attention. It is only nowadays that we see students—a small portion of them—playing in fields. It is no matter for surprise that we see, in India, that the intellectual giants are physical dwarfs.

At an English university, the regular course begins from the first of October and continues until the end of May, when it is closed for the summer holidays. Regular teaching by the professors forms only a small part. Students are expected to learn more by themselves. For instance, in the diploma course, we had only three half days for lectures but three full days for practise. We were asked to teach in different schools, under the supervision of the professors of the university. Notes of lessons had to be prepared and studied well beforehand, but we were not allowed to use them in the course of teaching the classes as they were taken by the supervisors. Demonstration classes by experienced teachers were given to train us in the art of teaching. Regarding the selection of subjects, there is no compulsion. Students are not asked to take subjects for which they have no liking or bent. The beautiful paintings and drawings of Miss G. Ismail tempted me to learn that art in this old age. While deciding about my additional subject, I boldly said that I wanted to take drawing, not having an idea of the standard of that art in diploma classes. They asked me whether I had taken drawing in lower classes. But my reply was, 'I shall do my best to learn that art as I have a great desire for it.' Once, when I was illustrating the village life of farmers in India on a chart, I had to draw bulls, ploughs, and men, showing how they were being used. Drawing, unfortunately, was never learnt by me as it had never been a part of my education. When I was labouring over a picture of a bull, Professor Smith entered the class. After going round he came and stood behind me and asked me what I was drawing, pointing to the figure I was struggling with. I told him that it was to be a bull but the head was not yet drawn. He said, 'Does it look like a pig?' I could not help laughing and preferred to display my ignorance than to cheat him, so I said, 'What a world of difference there is between a bull and a pig!' He smiled, saying there was no indication of a bull in my drawing and suggested to me that I might change my additional subject and asked what I would like to take instead. I said music, so I was asked to try it for a week. In England, they follow certain principles which are not adopted rigidly but subordinated to the interest and capacity of the students. But, here in India, every one of us must know the annual rainfall in Greenland, the number of wives Henry the VIII married, not to speak of several other details in every subject under the sun.

The aim at the University of Leeds, as of the others in European countries, is not to send out students with swollen heads stuffed with all kinds of information, but to develop their powers of mind and body and to fit them for their duties in later life, to give them a practical knowledge of life as fit citizens. They rightly understood that such a knowledge of life and men cannot be had within classrooms but by association with fellow students and participation in the social and athletic fields of activity.

You may ask me how the universities in England achieve this aim. As soon as a student joins the university he is given the following hints for his conduct at the university.

1. He is told that he is not going to be taught everything. He is asked to have his eyes open and learn things by himself. The university handbook and the notice boards are his only guides.

2. He is taught the value of societies and told that societies do not require sleeping partners. He is asked to take an active interest in the conduct of these societies with determination and enthusiasm. He is taught that determination brings with it enthusiasm; that he is not to be satisfied with a mere degree; that university education and culture, and not merely a degree, should be his aim.

3. He is taught to take an active part in all athletic activities of the university and also in public activities. The value of exercises and the cooperation involved in them is clearly impressed on his mind.

There are many associations, clubs, and societies. In India, only very few students take part in such activities. The cause lies in the system of education in India. Classes work continuously from 11 a.m. to 5 p.m. with a short interval of one hour in the middle. Societies and associations meet at intervals of at least a month and such meetings take place after 5 p.m.. Naturally, the students feel exhausted after the day's toil and are eager to go home. Most of them are poor and, therefore, cannot afford to have any lunch in the interval. What interest can they take in any activities when they are both tired and hungry? Added to these, our students do not get that encouragement from their teachers to induce them to take part in such activities. Our teachers must take greater interest in them and must not tenaciously stick to one particular class and must mix with the students much more freely. They must induce them to talk in such meetings so that, over the course of time, they may shake off their shyness. At English universities, one will see students competing with one another in academic discussions. Time does not permit me to speak about all the associations and societies they have at Leeds University. I shall just mention a few to give you an idea of how students are trained there.

1. There is a Debating Society which has its regular fortnightly meetings. The subjects are announced sufficiently early to enable intending partakers to prepare well. But, in India, students are generally informed only a day or two before the meeting. In England, they have inter-university debates in which delegates from different universities take part, and inter-hostel debates, with both girls and boys. But, in all such debates, professors take an active part and will be seen hidden behind the boys. The boys preside and run the society.

2. They have an Aeronautical Society in which topics relating to aircraft are discussed. Representatives of leading firms of aircraft, and those well known as civil

aviators, are invited to give talks to university students. In India, more than 90 per cent of the students know nothing of aviation.

3. There is the Church of England's Society for the purpose of bringing together the different members of the Church into closer union. The students are taught their responsibilities to the Church and their interest in religion is deepened. Annual university prayers and lectures on religious topics by prominent persons are arranged. Annual SCM weeks are observed when the students earn money by helping others; this money is used to buy clothes and other things for the poor and for the children of the servants.

4. They have the Conservative Society which provides for study and discussion of current political topics among students. Thus, students are prepared for national service after their career. With Indian students, politics is a forbidden fruit. Lectures here, by patriots, are permitted by educational authorities only on the assurance, 'no politics'. It is no wonder that a student gets his degree, and does not know who the present viceroy of India is. I am told that most of the applicants interviewed recently by the committee for the appointment of revenue probationers—MA's & MSC's exhibited colossal ignorance when questioned about current events.

5. There is the Dramatics Society, which meets weekly and where plays are read. Such meetings begin with tea and

are attended by both the staff and students. Every year, a play is enacted which is attended by the public also. The amount realized is utilized for the extension and improvement of the university.

6. They have the Historical and the Economical Society which gives sufficient scope for students to understand the social and economic problems of the times. It brings students interested in commerce and economics into close contact with leading professional businessmen who lecture to them on current problems.

7. There is a Photographic Society which organizes lantern lectures by authorities on photography. Demonstrations in photographic processes, enlargement, and development are given by professionals who are invited for the purpose. Many, among Indian students, may not even know the principles of photography. All their time is spent in knowing the heights of mountains and the lengths of rivers.

8. They also have a Music and Art Society with a view to developing among the students of the university, their aesthetic taste. There are two sections, the orchestral and choral, which meet almost every week. Weekly demonstrations are held for the benefit of the staff, the students, and the public. Musicians of high order and proficiency are invited at the cost of the University to give demonstrations. This side is positively discouraged in India, by the parents of our students, as tending to alienate them from their studies and treated as one not

forming part of their cultural development. But, abroad, it forms an integral part of the university course.

I am afraid I am boring you by giving a catalogue of the several societies and associations working at an English university. My object in so doing is to acquaint you with the manifold activities with which students at an English university are engaged. Their activities are not confined within the four walls of the university. They observe a hospital 'rag' day when they go into the city with boxes and collect money for the cause of the poor people in the hospitals and infirmaries. People, when they see ladies begging in the group, donate liberally. Thus, in 1934, they were able to collect a sum of £500 in one day. The boxes are opened by the secretary of the committee and the collections are sent to the local infirmary. I was told that the girls collected more money than the boys.

They observe a bazaar day, when students send something or other made by them. These things are exhibited in rooms. The day is advertised far and wide and on that day the opening ceremony is performed by a prominent person who gives a liberal donation; the exhibits are purchased by the public, staff, and students while the things remaining are auctioned to the students themselves. On this bazaar day in December 1934, they got a sum of £350 which was given away in aid of the library which was under construction.

A students' fund is collected to which the students, the staff of the university, and also the sympathetic public contribute for the purpose of affording financial assistance to students of the university. The award from the fund is not made to freshers but only to those who, having entered the university, are unable to continue without such assistance. The fund is administered by a small committee of students.

During holidays the students of the university visit villages nearby and engage themselves in rural reconstruction work. They talk to villagers, study their conditions, and give them the advice necessary for their improvement. Rural reconstruction work gives young educated men much scope to public service. These young enthusiasts do more service to the country than politicians who make loud speeches supporting this agreement or that fact, but who cut no ice. This kind of activity is woefully prevalent among our students. They think that they form an exclusive unit and do not concern themselves with others. In fact, they think that such public activities do not form a part of their education.

I must say something about the management and working of the hostels. There are four halls at the University of Leeds. Each hall has a warden, a sub-warden, a matron, and ten to fifteen maids. Each hall has a committee of twelve students who are elected by votes. The president of the committee is a senior student. This committee meets every week, and a general meeting for all the students is held once a month, when all questions relating to the management of the hall are discussed. Students are at liberty to bring, to the notice of the committee, any defect in the working of the hostel. Invariably, with the help of the warden, these defects are rectified and the needs of the students are provided. The entire management is, thus, left in the hands of students and, thus, they are trained in the art of organization.

The servants employed in these halls are all women. Male visitors are allowed to see the students on weekdays in the visitors' room and are not allowed to stay after 7 p.m. The main door of the hall is closed at 10 p.m.; students desirous of going to the cinema go in groups. A senior student becomes responsible to take the key from the warden and returns it back as soon as they return. Drinking is strictly prohibited on all occasions, both in the halls and at the university. I have heard many students, both men and women, say that they have never tasted liquor in their lives.

Hostels hold social functions such as: staff at home, friends at home, and freshers at home when the entire staff and the vice chancellor are invited to a grand tea party. After tea, a short concert is given by the students. During the annual Freshers' Social, a grand supper is arranged and the freshers are entertained by the old students. To create a spirit of tolerance in the newcomers they are teased during the course of the entertainment. Hostel dances are arranged twice a year when the warden and the sub-warden receive visitors from 6.30 to 7 p.m. The dance begins at 7 p.m. and lasts until 12 midnight. For supper, cold drinks and sweets are provided.

Such, in brief, is the training that is given to students in England. You will see how it is opposed to the system of education that prevails in India. In India, students are trained to develop only one side, the intellectual side. The education given to our students is, thus, defective, narrow, and one-sided. The aim of Indian education is not to fit students to circumstances of the ever-changing environment of the world, nor to enable them to contribute towards the progress and prosperity of their country, so the training pays no attention to achieve the ideal.

I do not mean to say that the system prevailing in England is perfect, but there is an honest attempt towards giving the right sort of training to students. Students in England are made to develop not only their intellectual faculty but also their social, physical, moral, and aesthetical senses. The educationists in India must put their heads together to devise a common system of training for our students with a view to turning out fit citizens and to fusing a link between school and university life, and life after the completion of education. Reduction of too many subjects, and specialization in one, at university is indispensable. The present Indian system has made the students beginners in all subjects and masters of none.

More freedom should be given to the students to mix with their teachers so that this sense of inferiority could be replaced by power, expression, assertion, and independent-thinking among them. In England, a student does not feel a sense of inferiority in the company of teachers. They are made to feel that the university is a spacious garden which every student is expected to dress and take care of. The main aim of the university in England is not to teach but to open the vision of the students to the conditions and needs of men, to enable them to think and act independently, and to be guided by their own convictions. The subjects taught are not treated as ends, but as tools, for a larger purpose.

An English university serves as a guide to the life of man and, unlike India, prevents the terrible waste of labour and talent.

26

Women of East and West
in Cooperation

Address at the International Women's Twelfth World Congress, held at Istanbul, 4 September 1935

The world is becoming a neighbourhood; the old barriers of time and space have broken down. The old isolations are rapidly disappearing. What is spoken or done in one part of the world is known in a few hours in a very distant part. No region can live long unto itself. The East, hitherto remote and self-contained, is now finding herself in the stream of the world's life and thoughts. Hence, the ideas, the opinions, the activities of one part of the world are vital to every other part. New international problems are constantly arising and new causes of friction developing. Thoughtful people see that if civilization is to survive at all the people of this world must learn to live together in close contact and harmony. They must appreciate the contributions to human welfare, which every race has made and is making. They must understand the customs, ideals, and cultures of others and seek common interests and purposes.

The East is not 'the ancient unchanging East'. It is a modern East which has absorbed and assimilated, in its broad river of thought, a good deal that comes from other parts of the world. One must try to visualise the idea of this country, which was mature in thought before any of the nations of modern Europe were ever born, which has since grown further in spite of relapses, and which now stands before the world full of new hopes and aspirations, ready to offer what is hers to give and to receive what is yours to offer on the single condition that the offering and the receiving shall not be made an occasion for arguments of superiority and inferiority, or for compulsion. All gifts are best which are given and received in simplicity, in the spirit in which we take the blessing of nature and also her chastisement and correction.

The true inwardness of the human spirit can best be discovered in art. The history of art furnishes a most certain criterion of what people thought and felt in different ages. If you take the art of two countries or people at their best, you will be able to judge the essential characters of those countries or people more surely than if a conceited panegyrist or a prejudiced dictator was allowed to intervene. Art may also help to remove misunderstandings and enable diverse groups of humanity to work together for the progress of the whole human family. Music, a particular branch of art, is also helpful in bringing people together. And there is less understanding between Eastern and Western music than there need be. Many Eastern ears profess to be able to enjoy Western music, and many Westerners return the compliment in the converse sense. The difficulty lies in a failure to realize the separate historical development of each. It must be remembered that modern European music is barely four centuries old. On the other hand, Eastern music is not an undeveloped art but a highly developed art on different lines.

Religion plays such an important part in Eastern life that it is absolutely essential that we should give some attention to it in discussing the East with the rest of the world. In the West, religion is sharply distinguished from secular matters. It is possible for people to cooperate in most of the affairs of life without inquiring about each other's religion. At one time, religion was coextensive with life. Now, it has become the individual's private affair. My purpose in dealing with religion here is not to criticise, but to see whether any contrast that we find makes it impossible, in the first place, for the followers of the great religions to work together in all the great cultural movements of their countries. If we think clearly on this twofold task we find that not only is cooperation possible from both points of view, but that it is eminently desirable. We shall have helped to destroy a whole bundle of prejudices which stand in the way of human progress. In my view, the religion of all thinking beings is the same, however different may be the philosophy by which they explain their spiritual instincts or the moulds in which they cast their spiritual hopes.

When once this lesson is grasped by the people of the East and those of the West, they will be able to work together more efficiently for the good of humanity. If the Eastern people further realize that modernism in thought and action, in spiritual and material outlook, as evolved in the West, is a natural stage of evolution in which the whole of mankind has an interest, and to which the whole of mankind has contributed, there will be no obstacle to their taking their rightful place in the human quest for the highest truth, the truth that relates to our inmost spiritual being and our ultimate destiny in time and eternity. On the other hand, the religious experiences and spiritual cravings of the East have much in them that will help the thought of the modern West, as they have helped its thought in the past.

Leading modern educational thinkers in the West have already influenced Eastern education, and will doubtless do so to an even greater extent in the future. Much of what they teach has been scientifically tested and their educational systems have been greatly eulogized, and the East may profit by this body of educational truth if she relates it intelligently to her own life.

The Girl Guides Movement is undoubtedly an instrument of unity, harmony, and cooperation among the women of the world. The youth of over fifty nations have come under its beneficial influence. It has been acclaimed as the greatest educational experiment of the twentieth century. The fundamental principles and vital ideals on which the movement is based have universal appeal in themselves to all people, irrespective of race, colour, creed, and customs.

It is indispensable that the East should cooperate with the West for the improvement and development of this practical side of the education of our girls, who are privileged members of the future generation. The movement is still in its infancy in the East.

Child marriage and its harmful effects on the race and nation, prevention of widow marriages, unemployment, and unjust treatment of women in political, economic, and social life will lead to further decadence.

The legal rights and social customs of the East, especially in India, are so rigid that it seems hard to surmount them. But, in my view, it is not only Indians who have these difficulties but also the whole world in some way or the other. Otherwise, we would not have assembled here under the name of the IWW Congress. One essential is that we must make the whole world into one human family. The members of the family will not be happy, if one of them is suffering. This idea is beautifully expressed by a Persian poet, Sa'adi, when he says that if one portion of the body is suffering, the other parts feel the pain equally and acutely. We have to formulate certain rules and principles applicable to all the members of our family, irrespective of caste, creed, customs, colour, and religion.

Isolation is not good for the East. It is not open to her to isolate herself. She has sometimes tried to isolate herself in her past history, but isolation has always meant stagnation. There is a tendency among some of the men of India to seek a new kind of isolation. A narrow view of events makes them antagonistic to the West and its science, medicine, and civilization. To encourage this tendency is to plunge the East deeper in the mire. We all realize the shortcomings of Western civilization. They are realized nowhere more than in the modern West itself. What we ought to realize is that Western civilization is modern, built on the experiences of many centuries in the East and in the West. To turn away from it, as if it were something alien or hostile to us, is to misread the lessons of history. On the contrary, we ought to welcome in it all the seeds of progress and all the healthy elements that help to conquer, or subdue, the ailments to which any human system is liable.

I request the West, on its side, to understand the East in its past history and present aspirations. For a variety of reasons, false ideas of race or cultural superiority have gained ground, but on that score perhaps no nation or people or country has a right to cast the first stone in the new world to be. We want to use every agency: political, economic, educational, and social to prevent false ideas from dominating the intercourse of the people. The choicest spirits and the noblest teachers have always realized and taught the brotherhood of man. We must bring that idea home to the women in the street and the women in the marketplace.

Our objective is a high one; we should not be discouraged with our present conditions. There is no progress without effort; the more educative, it is the more joy it gives and the more happy memories it leaves behind. The essential thing is to have faith in our ideals. There is a great deal of that true spirit of encouragement in the following lines:

Duty whispers low, 'Thou must', and faith replies, 'I can'.

27

Progress of Women's Education Abroad

A speech delivered under the auspices of the Muhammadan Educational Association of South India under the chairmanship of Mr Little-Wiles, Vice Chancellor of Madras University

The progress of women's education in foreign countries such as England, Turkey, Egypt, Switzerland, and Germany (before Hitlerism came into existence) is really amazing. Education of women there is psychologized and socialized, and is carried out with a definite purpose, that of developing her character, making her independent, and enabling her to serve the nation. Education is adapted to the character and needs of the people. A regard for past traditions, cultures, and principles is not quite absent. The civilization is not imitative but is real and unique—the outcome of the needs felt by the people themselves. Hence, it is creative and useful. There is no gap or divergence between the civilized and uncivilized women. There is an understanding and cooperation of each other's ideals and ideas. Even the old women who are a drag on the progress of young girls here, are changing, progressive, and active there. There, one finds all, old and young, busy in something, planning, scheming, and consciously or unconsciously working for the progress of the nation. One is hardly ever in a position to hear idle talk or a scandal among those ladies, both old and young. Very often, the cry is heard that there is no time for them to do all that they want to do, but our women find so much time that they do not know how to pass it.

A visitor entering a school or college (in the morning) will see a group of girls with peculiar uniforms and tools working in the school garden and in the orchard, some of them digging, some cultivating, and some collecting fruits, leaves, flowers, and vegetables. The visitor will also notice that large and small plants are evenly spread in straight rows and each row uniformly planned. The sense of neatness and beauty in the workers is so great that the garden is made heavenly. She will be told by the teacher responsible that there are common and individual gardening plots. The girls are fully responsible for the individual plots and they have to work for certain hours in the day on the common plot. Each girl has a register and she has to enter an account of the success or failure of the crop, the causes of success, and the remedy to prevent failure. The accounts of the expenditure and the benefit derived by sales are also kept by the students. Classroom instruction in nature study is followed by experimentation on the plot system.

This practical side of education in all girls' schools is given preference to theoretical teaching. Handwork forms an important item in the curriculum. The aim is to make the pupils (especially backward ones) understand an abstract thought by means of construction, and to add reality to every subject in the curriculum. Consultation classes are held in the mornings when girls bring ideas of the object they want to construct. They draw it, and its design is decorated with colours to be used in the model. The idea originates in the child's environment, and ways and means for production are thereafter sought by her. The object is made through her own efforts. There are different kinds of industries in every school. Girls are not compelled to join one and leave the other. A girl can take to any industry she likes. Provision is made for making dresses, hats, carpets, cushions, bedroom slippers, dust rugs, and many other things that are used in daily life. The articles are made to supply the demands of the people of the neighbourhood. Emphasis is laid on the aesthetic side of the object, and economy in the use of materials. Records of finished articles, the price of each, and the time taken for it are kept by individual students.

Book binding, book repairing, and the framing of pictures are often taught. One group of students cuts and trims pages, another group make holes in them, a third group will be sewing all the pages in the form of a book, while a fourth group will paste cloth and fasten and finish the work.

Domestic science is given equal importance in almost all schools. A group of girls will be seen busily preparing a lunch for the whole school. Each girl is made responsible for preparing a certain dish or for certain work. She has to produce an account of her work; if a dish is spoilt, then why and for what reason; if it is well prepared, then what was the method that she used. Records of the ingredients used, the price of each, the cost of the whole dish, for how many persons it was made, and also the account of the whole lunch for all are shown in the records. In preparing meals, care is taken to provide all necessary vitamins according to the age, health, and variety of work of the students.

The canteen system is not an uncommon thing in such schools. This is managed by the pupils of the higher class. They have a real shop with all necessary commodities used by both the teachers and the taught. Even articles for industrial classes are provided by them. The group in charge of this is allowed to go to market once a week to find out prices, and to buy whatever is necessary. Goods in the school shop are sold at market rates so no one cares to go to other shops outside the school. Another group will be seen working in the same department, whose duty it is to keep records of the things bought and sold, to write letters, sales slips, bills of goods, advertisements, and posters. These groups work in rotation.

Many schools have opened dispensaries. A group of girls attend it in the afternoon on working days, and on holidays both in the morning and evening. Fees for treating rich girls of the school and outsiders from the neighbourhood are taken, as are contributions for the 'Dispensary Poor Box'. The money is used for the purpose of buying medicines. Simple ailments are treated. The disease is studied by the girls and the treatment is written in consultation with the teacher. The girl responsible for a certain ailments study must keep a record of her work, the kind of disease, the treatment, the changes she has noticed while treating it, the period the patient took to get cured, and the amount she charged. The group is allowed to go to local dispensaries to acquire further knowledge and instruction. Local doctors are requested to visit the school dispensaries and give advice. A first aid class has been started in the lower classes and big sized dolls are used for practise. The part played by the teacher, in all practical classes, is almost nothing. She will be seen as one of the members of the group, sometimes working with the group and sometimes with an individual.

Another striking institution is the opening of a cooperative credit society. Students are encouraged to save money from their allowances or earnings in the industrial section. All of them deposit a part of their savings in the school bank. The money thus realized is invested in different industrial sections, not only in the school but also outside. Simple and compound interest is calculated once a year and the depositors are given an interest of 20 per cent. Loans are granted to poor girls to enable them to continue their studies. This group is taken, quarterly, to public banks to study the methods used in depositing and withdrawing money. The school bank is run on similar lines. One should remember that all these things are done by the girls themselves, with no cause for complaint, and done so exquisitely, promptly, accurately, and honestly that even men of certain other countries could not excel in such work.

Self-government, as the natural corollary of self–development, begins in schools and is successfully continued in colleges. A students' council is elected consisting of six to eight girls. The duty of the council is to organize and supervise the committees in charge of school duties. The committees are also elected and the teacher's consent taken. There are as many committees as there are duties. Their function is to uphold the discipline of the students, to improve the industries already mentioned, to see to the sanitation and cleanliness of the school, and to supervise the hostel entertainments, games, and sports, the care of the sick, and the helping of small girls. Misbehaviour and any cases of mischief are referred to the students' council which discusses such matters and decides on appropriate punishment. The head of the school gets a report of the student's work and, in consultation with the other teachers, any punishment is usually carried out. It was said that the decision of the students' council was rarely overlooked as it was invariably most considerate and lenient.

Physical culture, from the beginning of the school career right up to college, is made compulsory. Provision for the same is fully adequate. Equipment is provided, teachers are trained, refresher courses are given to them to keep them up-to-date with the scientific methods of physical training. Every teacher is a teacher of physical culture. She keeps an eye on the students in the class or in industries with a view to correcting their posture. Physical culture is also meant to aid the development of intellect and character. The girls become more efficient and are capable of greater activity.

The systematic training given to them has been a great help in effecting a harmonious bodily development. Games are not neglected. These are encouraged in different ways. Since they stimulate a spirit of true and brave sportsmanship, the house system compels all girls to take part in such games. Inter-school and inter-collegiate matches develop a spirit of unity among them. Swimming, folk dancing, classical dancing, riding, and gymnasium feats are all taught and loved by the students.

The drama is another very important item in the student's life. Generally, the English composition period includes drama. The teacher knows that a certain ballad, story, or poem is appreciated by the girls. So, she takes it and asks the students to compose sentences. These are noted down on the blackboards and when they constitute something like a scene, the girls are made to act it. In higher classes, historical events or stories are enacted. The choice of a story, the time, place, language, dress and scenic effects are all left to the creative ability of the girls. In colleges, classical plays or those written by the foremost English playwrights are acted. Dramatization has a very great educative value. It helps the players to be physically fit, it corrects their posture, it encourages them to be bold and to fit their talk to their action.

What are the social, intellectual, economic, and political conditions of women of those countries? They are certainly far better than ours. Their fight for equal rights and status began long before we thought of it. They have not only got all they wanted but have also been making good use of their liberty. The women of those countries, particularly those of Turkey, have carried the torch of reform and have set a living example for us. They are either members or presidents of numerous associations started in the interests of womenfolk. Such associations are, for example, the Union of Turkish Women, the Association for Raising the Intellectual Standard of Women, the Administrative Council, the Red Crescent of Faith, the National Economy Committee, the Temperance Association, the Committee for Helping the Poor, the State Education Committee, the Committee for Child Protection, the Mothers' Union, the Turkish Republic Committee, and the Complete Equality Committee. Women are members of all these associations. They work with men in other departments, such as those of the railway, postal, navy, police, judiciary, electric and telephone, and last and not the least they assist the military department. They are trained to join all these departments as recruits and cadets. One will find them working dauntlessly along with the men. Their zeal, energy, enthusiasm, and activity seem in no way inferior to that of men. There is a strong spirit of cooperation, determination, and excellence in them. Whatever they do, they do it promptly and accurately. They teach one another and learn one from the other. Their leisure time is spent in rational amusement. They have a developed power of judgement, which helps them to appreciate what is good and to deprecate what is evil in character. Individual interests are subordinated to those of the whole nation. In short, they are resourceful and self-possessed, so that they are in a position to overcome personal disabilities.

Co-education in Turkey has been very successful. It begins from primary education and continues up to university. In many institutions, the heads of colleges are ladies. They say they have absolutely no difficulty in running such institutions. The idea of marriage is not the only means of support for ladies abroad. The goal of their lives is all round excellence and development of all their faculties. The success of co-education in Turkey is partly due to the strict observance of Islamic principles which forbid familiarity or illicit relations between men and women, and is also due to the highly developed character, the strong sense of self-respect, and the dignified personality which is found among Turkish women.

The social condition of ladies in foreign countries is quite different from that existing in this country. They have subordinated their social dispositions to intellectual reasoning. They are not the slaves of old customs and traditions, but have brought about a revolution in them. A dynamic attitude to life, an appreciation of human virtues, and the elimination of shortcomings is conspicuously prominent in their mode of life. Such reforms were not imposed upon them but its need was felt by them themselves and they successfully achieved its realization.

28

Muslim Women's Education

A lecture given before the Muslim Society of Great Britain, at London, 2 February 1935

I am very thankful to the Muslim Society of Great Britain for the honour conferred upon me by asking me to talk. This is my first opportunity of speaking to a gathering of men. I do not know whether I will be able to express my ideas as forcibly as I would do to an audience of women. I need not tell you how nervous I feel among you. I rely entirely on your indulgence to deal with me leniently if I fall short of your expectations.

The subject of women's education is a very vast one. If I have to do justice to it, I must divide it into two parts. The first will deal with the necessity of education and the second with the scheme of education. I shall deal with the first part as I have come across many Muslims who are labouring under the misconception that education for our girls is unnecessary. I am afraid my introductory remarks, as to the necessity of such education, may be very outspoken and even sensational from the orthodox Muslim point of view. I feel that open and frank statements are much more effective than insidious lip service under the cover of praise and sympathy. I hope my apparent platitudes will be pardoned in view of the great cause before us.

Woman as a social unit, is as social a being as a man. The gregarious instinct in us is so great that it compels us to be in the company of not only the members of the same sex but also those of the opposite sex. Hence, if a society is to be prosperous, progressive, and happy it must have a reasonable amount of free mixing of both the sexes as we have been seeing here in the society of the most advanced nations of the world. Its development as a whole depends upon the harmonious development of its parts. But, in Muslim society, a man or woman belonging to it, not being very well acquainted with the characteristics of the other sex, is mentally and morally dwarfed and is unfit to successfully tackle the problems of the modern world.

Woman, as an individual, has the same power of feeling, sentiment, and emotions as a man. The faculties of mind, such as observation, reasoning, criticism, and power of expression grow in a child from a very young age and, at the age of five or six, a child feels an impelling force within to express itself in different ways. It may be by talking or by writing letters. The lectures and speeches delivered by so many men are the results of this impelling force within, which compels them to accept such opportunities, so this power is not altogether absent even in elderly men. Composition through drawing and painting or music and even dancing—these are different forms of its expression— is conducive to happiness and satisfaction, and its denial leads to misery and unhappiness. Women are susceptible to the joys and sorrows of this world to the same extent as men. They, like men, continually fall prey to the ills of existence. They have to encounter, in the battlefield of this world, the same amount of evil as men. If philosophy is a solace of mind to a man, it is the same to a woman. If he takes interest in literary pursuits, she also takes an interest as keenly if she is given the same opportunity and facility. But, for reasons incomprehensible to me, they have been treated as reasonless beings and incapable of following a course of action that would be of benefit to humanity. Is it not the greatest delight, for us humans, to do great services which contribute to the well-being of the whole of humanity? Women are better fitted to achieve this end. They are endowed with gentleness of manner, persuasive power, and they take delight in succouring misery. Is it right that they should be deprived, by men, of almost every opportunity of exercising the great powers they possess? If you could know the feelings of many millions of women, you would find they are miserable because they never had fair opportunity given to them. They have a right to demand that the gifts which have been bestowed upon them by their Maker should not be arbitrarily taken away simply because they are called women, and that they should not be shut out from what is good and great in the world.

In the theatre of the world, and especially in that of the illiterate Muslim world, women are treated as puppets; they live not for themselves but for their autocratic men of unlimited power. We have seen women of other nations play as important a part in the activities of this world as a man. A great thinker says,

> We are foolish and without excuse foolish in speaking of the superiority of one sex to the other as if they can be compared in similar ways. Each has what the other has not and each completes the other and is completed by the other. They are in nothing alike and the happiness and perfection of both depends on each asking and receiving from the other what only the other can give.

These are the words of a great thinker. What is it that a woman can give to a man? Woman is an embodiment of love, affection, care, and tenderness, and she can claim all the moral characteristics. What is that a man can give to a woman? He can support her by his physical courage, candour, and patience in facing the difficulties of the world, and has the instinct of discipline.

The modern thinking Indian will surely admit that education is that which develops the mental faculties and serves to maintain discipline among them. Those who have undergone a certain discipline are capable of adapting themselves to any condition of life—happy or miserable, favourable or prejudicial. The fundamental fact of life is that this is a hard world and living is hard for all creatures but specially for the least evolved and for those unadjusted to their conditions. Right education is disinterested and it brings up the woman for her own sake and for the sake of her race, nation, and country.

Although men and women are naturally under obligation morally, physically, and spiritually to each other, the wonder is that it is not brought home to them in all the experiences of their daily lives. Yet, how evident is the simple truth that men and women need to depend on each other in order to derive happiness through the proper performance of their mutual duties? They still need more to repair the natural defects of each other by means of contact and culture. As the natural roughness of man's nature, if left to itself, develops into cruel barbarity making him unfit for domestic life, so does the natural weakness, helplessness, and backwardness of woman if kept in its original state become a source of constant discomfort to both the sexes. Of course, it is not possible to do away with the weakness of women altogether, but it is the duty of every sensible member to try and effect as much improvement in this direction as lies in his or her power.

For a nation to be brave, true, and noble, its women should be taught so first. The destiny of a nation lies far more in the hands of women since, within the house, the power of the mother reigns supreme in many spheres and, though they may be weak individually, they are strong collectively. The uneducated mothers are often themselves mere children in intellect with nothing to teach their little ones but fabulous legends and old world superstitions. Since the imagination is very strong in early years, the mother's teaching, however foolish, leaves an indelible impression stamped on children's minds. The earthly rewards and punishment of worthy and unworthy men are to a great extent in the hands of women. We must care for women who are the educators of the human race if we desire the new generation to accomplish its work. It is the parents' examples, words, and manners which form the child's character far beyond any mere verbal instruction. The Muslim people, who carried off the palm for bravery, hospitality, generosity, intellect, and skill, have abused all these wonderful qualities and have now degenerated into idleness, ignorance, bigotry, sensuality, and pride. The degeneration, demoralisation, and denaturalisation of our community is the direct cause of the illiterate womanhood and their theoretical and practical fatalism and religious formalism. National excellence depends upon the culture and discrimination of women.

The spread of education among women is indispensable both for the sake of family happiness and national progress. There is a strong desire in both sexes for each other's comradeship. The newly married husband, too, feels the craving for his wife's companionship in everything that concerns and interests him. In the course of time, he learns that due to unfavourable customs or lack of culture in his wife, she is unfit to participate in all the phases of his life. He gives up this idea in despair and tries to develop friendships with women of other nations who seem better fitted to be of interest to him. Many young men have frantically been trying to produce hybrids in blood on the plea that our girls are ill-educated and so incapable of making their lives happy. I would say, though, that our girls are illiterate but not uneducated. I don't like to lay much emphasis on this lame excuse as I have seen hundreds of men, after their Western education who are not only living a happy life with their old-fashioned wives but who have also brought about reform in their homes. This is the meaning of real education. Education should not be a means of creating a big cleavage between the educated and the uneducated but it should be an instrument of unity and harmony among people. It should serve to supply the needs and necessities of the home, society, and country. In this connection, I would only say that our poor young men, living in the present to whom the past and the future mean nothing, sometimes act, like lunatics. They lack strong willpower and firmness of character. Character is the pivot on which the whole value of a person hinges; a woman's character is her strength, strength for her future progress and development. We have seen that there are four fundamental factors for the development of one's character—the home, the school, the church, and the society. All these fundamental factors have been, day and night, trying to develop one aspect of life. Unfortunately, such an important thing has been neglected by us. Our homes are disorganized centres of quarrels, our schools are good for nothing, our society simply does not exist, and our mosques are monopolized by our selfish men on the plea that they are polluted by the presence of women. Thus, when the deeper motives and higher principles of life are either ignored or are made secondary, how can nobleness and high mindedness result? Good grain must be sown even though it may be apparently unproductive for a time. Some day it will put forth a blade and come into ear. When the need comes, the growth will be rapid.

Our young men should determine to see the women of their community as more than the progenitors of children. Women's duty is not only the perpetuation of the race but to be real Muslim mothers with the inheritance of bravery, patience, forbearance, and love, to see that they are the fittest preceptors and educators of their children; so, we must see that our girls draw nourishment not only from English fairy tales but also take delight in the lives of our own heroes and heroines. The Muhammadan concept of the complete seclusion of women has also carried countless evils in its train. The uneducated women have become, through ages of neglect, a prey to ignorance and superstitions and victims of men's selfishness. Yet, in spite of century after century of debasing customs, the higher ideals have never died away, even though outward conditions have altered and, in recent years, as we have seen with the revival of national life this ideal has come again to the front. The seclusion has undermined their health, has made them an economic burden, has made their education difficult, and has crammed, narrowed, and repressed their personalities. The intrinsic worth of our women is very high and their outstanding qualities are dignity, repose, idealism, modesty, courtesy, hospitality, love of children, devotion to religion, and a spirit of sacrifice. These wonderful qualities have been aspired to by the women of other countries. I would, unhesitatingly, say that those who oppose the education of women are not the friends of humanity but they are wicked enemies of the human race at large wherever they may be.

Unfortunately, the word 'education' itself is misinterpreted and is mistaken for the passing of examinations and acquiring of diplomas. Hence, it is concluded that it is necessary for teachers and for poor girls who have to earn their living. The real meaning of the word is as follows.

Every child comes into the world with an equipment of inborn tendencies and capacities which tend to call forth certain responses to certain stimuli. The baby will cry out because of discomfort or pain. He will, in time, reach out for bright objects. These he will manipulate and he will make exploratory movements, moving his arms and legs vigorously. He will manifest anger, fear, or tendencies depending upon the stimuli used. These tendencies are highly modifiable and they are conditioned by environmental contact. He learns to associate the milk bottle with food if the bottle is given to him. He associates food with crying. If, upon making a definite sound, a certain satisfaction recurs he will give that sound whenever he wants that satisfaction. In this way, a whole series of new responses may be built into the child's mental mechanism.

Two things are clearly involved: the child and the environment, and in their interaction changes take place in both. Environmental stimuli are constantly changing and so is the child. New adjustments need to be made. The tendency maybe to respond, in a certain way, to an environmental situation but, when it is found that the situation has slightly changed and the old response does not fit, it is necessary to modify the old response. These modifications and interconnections become more and more complex as life continues, especially if the person retains, to a large degree, the power of adjusting himself to new situations, ideas, and contacts. The modifying of these tendencies and responses in an individual is what is known as 'education' and the process of making such changes is 'learning'. Hence, a person may be illiterate but not uneducated.

I feel that I must give credit to the young men of this century who seem full of enthusiasm and spirit for the revival of their national life. Their philanthropic work is indispensable for the regeneration of our community. Recently, I was speaking to a young friend of mine in whom I found an inborn aptitude to serve humanity. Our talk was on the abolition of the purdah system. He, in his youthful ardour, mentioned what he was going to do after his return. The scheme laid for this achievement was a very simple one and, of course, not very thoughtful. It was just to induce some of his friends to bring their sisters out of their homes. But, the future of those poor illiterate girls, who are so ill-acquainted with the character of the other sex, has not yet been considered by him. But, when such reformative spirits unite they can do wonders. Personally, I am not for revolution as revolutions destroy too much, even though they may be productive for the time being. In the end, they are very harmful. Any progress or growth, if it is to be real and sure, must be gradual and slow.

I end my talk with one sentence. A cultured mother is not only the fittest preceptor and educator of her children, she is also a constant source of delight to them when she is educated.

29

Character and Education

Character is the crown of one's life and it is the pivot upon which the whole personality of a person is built up. It is the source of one's progress, success, and happiness in life. It is a matter of growth from within and is acquired by one's own efforts irrespective of worldly position. It is made up from a life of contact and self-discipline. It is the controlled self, by the organization of one's instincts and sentiments into the master sentiments. It is strong when the organization is close and comprehensive; it is weak when there are loose ends lying about. It is the sum total of the native basis of disposition and temperament which varies in different people of different races. They are the motive power of all thought and action. They are favoured or checked to a certain extent by social circumstances, environment, and training.

Modern educationists have been professing to regard character as the best aspect of human life, but actual practise has not borne out such a profession. The fact is character has been too narrowly interpreted, its intellectual, emotional, and moral aspects have been insufficiently recognized, and it has been, too lightly, taken for granted as an automatic product of a time-honoured system. Any specific attempt in that direction has been considered as superfluous on account of it not producing quick returns that can readily be measured.

If we only recognize that the training of character is to form certain habits, whether intellectual, emotional, or moral, we come to a definite understanding as to what we mean by 'character'. These habits may be lasting or temporary. The formation of them needs a constant and vigilant watch, and a careful study of methods adopted in adjustment of means to ends and their reaction on the taught. It also should be remembered that the different sides of character cannot be dissociated in practise, but they can be involved in the task of establishing discipline which should not be external and repressive.

What is the relationship between character and intelligence, and how is intellectual character formed? Mental faculties, such as the power of observation, imagination, reasoning, thinking, and judgement, begin from the very early age of three or four. And, the instincts of curiosity, constructiveness, and combativeness also develop side by side. Children feel an impelling force within to express themselves in different ways, to act, and to construct things. Expression and construction in different forms are conducive to satisfaction and happiness. If opportunities and facilities are logically and systematically provided to children to express themselves freely, and independently, the mental faculties develop. If a good foundation is laid, and a good taste for reading and thoughtful study is created, they will be in a position to increase their knowledge by their own efforts in later life. But, no logical and systematic; development of the instincts is attempted either at home or at school; hence, the results of primary schools are somewhat disappointing. In later years, the early curiosity is lost and the instruments of acquiring knowledge, not being put to a profitable use, begin to decay. The development of intellect mostly depends upon sympathetic treatment on the calm, healthy, happy condition of their minds, upon making the matter as simple as possible to be understood by the children. While developing intellectual character, one should try to understand the motives, interests, and instincts of the children and try to work with them and not against them. The instincts are the greatest ally of an educator.

The formation of lasting intellectual habits needs particular attention both by parents and teachers. These are formed in one's own life when one is in the stage of preparing for the art of life. But, in actual practise, it is difficult to form genuine habits as life, both at home and at school is made as artificial as possible. The artificiality of life does not help the powers of the mind to be lively and habitual. Hence, both young and old live a dual form of life. One is the real life in which they can express themselves freely and independently by following their own instincts. The other is by submitting themselves to a regime which seems to them as arbitrary and hindering in their efforts at self-expression. Hence, reward and punishment, praise and blame, and various appeals to the spirit of competition, as an incentive to effort, have been advised and used. These, no doubt, serve a temporary purpose but they cannot produce lasting intellectual habits as things done from external motives do not necessarily become habits having an effect on life. The result is that people are devoid of intellect. Even those who have developed the so-called intellect in their school careers relapse into intellectual apathy after leaving it. This is due to their not having undergone some fundamental change during their developing stage. The fact is that people, after completing their educational career, are left to themselves, without external influences, to direct their intellect or make an intellectual effort by themselves; hence, they take leave of all their motives for intellectual effort.

What is most essential is to bring education and reality into line with each other by establishing a connection between instincts and learning. This may produce some difficulties owing to differences between individuals and subjects but a great deal of resourcefulness, imagination, and sympathy on the part of teachers and parents will solve the problem. All creative activities do bring education into line. Theoretical education leaves very little chance for the formation of intellectual channels. Every step, in the imparting of knowledge, should be accompanied by practise, illustration, personal taste, or hobbies. The readiness of the teachers and parents to meet children halfway may profoundly influence their attitude towards further education. Some educationists advocate an almost unlimited degree of freedom to children. But, this is not advisable as children cannot be treated from the outset as if they possess mature judgement, experience, and self-knowledge. No doubt they are rational beings. The purpose of any educator, worthy of the name, should be to make children clearly understand the end and the object of the work. If it is put in an intrinsic, rather than an extrinsic, form it will be within their powers of comprehension. Children cannot understand the far off end. It may be considered that every stage of work cannot be made interesting. People do not hesitate to do any hard work if they know the purpose of it. The same is the case with children. It does not mean that the teacher, in order to make the work interesting, should try to make them shirk difficult work. The present system of providing students with printed notes has resulted in disaster, it has produced decay of their intellectual powers, has cramped their personalities and suppressed their powers of expression. It will probably be admitted that, while forming intellectual habits, drudgery will make the children unable to confront difficulties manfully and to persevere at dull work. Drudgery can easily be avoided by bringing into play dramatic performances, entertainments, displays, debates, short lectures by scholars, a school magazine, investigations into matters of local interest, the provision of various forms of equipment for the school, exhibitions, and such things as parents' day. These also help to make school life interesting and real.

It may be argued that children face drudgery from a sense of duty. This hard saying may cause an unreasonable strain on their minds. Grown-up people perform work involving drudgery, from a sense of duty, when they are satisfied that it serves some useful purpose. Children also will do the same when they are identified with a similar purpose. 'Reason proclaims my duty and my sense of duty impels me to do it'. Duty means precise devotion to various kinds of good in proportion to their relative value and importance. It is an impulse to action and comprises moral sentiment and the development of self-regarding sentiment. It enables one to judge rightly of the relative value of moral good and impels one to pursue the best. It can be acquired by any person, by a slow process of growth under the constant pressure of social environment and moral tradition.

Emotional character refines one's feelings and widens the personal range by providing worthy appeals and worthy outlets. There is no definite distinction between intellectual and emotional character. Intellect and emotions act and read upon each other. Intellectual development increases one's own aspirations and produces the sense of pleasure that accompanies the realization of a purpose and which is an inspiration to further efforts.

Creative activities, such as music, poetry, drawing, painting, rhythmic exercises, and handicrafts, do directly inspire and express special feelings and develop the attitude of creation and appreciation. Unluckily, some people take a strictly utilitarian view of education and belittle the influence of creative activities on the human mind. The means of living are indispensable but they are, after all, only means and not end. People are gradually realising that mere theoretical education is not everything and that they should be made to get more out of their lives. To raise the standard of living, one need not only to improve one's material conditions but one also requires fine feeling and the appreciation of beauty. Emotions inevitably play a great part in life. In connection with these, it is essential, as in other branches of education, to start from what the children already appreciate and understand.

Moral character is developed through environmental contact, mostly by the teacher, but also through everyday incidents of importance in the school and home life, such as mutual courtesy, cheerful obedience to duty, consideration, respect for others, and kindness to animals. These ideals leave an indelible impression on children's young minds. These cannot be inculcated by mere oral precepts but by the exercise and practise of them in daily life. That is what is required for the development of these qualities. Responsibility of certain work, entrusted to children, develops their sense of responsibility, inspires sufficient respect in them, and helps them to exact a high standard of behaviour from others. The sense of social responsibility is developed at home and at school. The school, being a large body, is an appropriate place to give its members the concept of collective life. It is small enough to bring it home to them that each one can play an important part for, or against, its interest. Social activities promote cooperation, power organization, sense of justice, fairness, responsibility, reasonableness, unselfishness, chivalry, and good temper. The games teach children how to bear themselves well, both as winners and losers, and develop a high degree of insight and wisdom in their application to social service.

There are certain things in which the development of moral character should be direct. Warning against intemperance, gambling, and theft carry conviction; a direct appeal to reason is possible as the harmful consequences of such habits are obvious. Cleanliness and order should be insisted upon from the outset. Teaching of morals against dishonesty and other similar faults which undermine character must be dogmatic. Instruction in them should be serious and definite. Even in religious instruction, definite warnings will develop personality and character. Mere negative teaching in such cases wearies the listener and provokes antagonism which defeats its own purpose.

Thus, we see that there is a close relationship between instincts, interests, motives, and education. Character is the sum total of them all. The educator can do much to foster the growth of worthy sentiments by holding them up as ideals to be achieved, by bringing education and reality into line, by bridging the gulf between school and home life. Character and education act and react upon each other. One without the other is a body without a soul.

30

The Educative Value of the Girl Guides Movement

The Girl Guides training commences when the girls are in the formative stage of mental, physical, and moral development. It creates opportunities for the full play of their spirit of adventure and service. Its system of games and practises make a wide appeal to girls of all communities, irrespective of their rigid social customs. It provides them with the healthy and useful companionship of girls of the same age, ideas, and ideals under the leadership of an experienced and active sister. It unites them all into a junior league of nations.

Guiding is the greatest factor for the development of one's character. Mere moral sentiments professed by teachers in classrooms do not constitute character. It is not an imposed object but an acquired ideal. It is acquired through environmental contact in one's daily life. It is formed by a life of self-discipline, self-sacrifice, and introspection. Genuine admiration for another's excellence acts as a powerful incentive in the formation of character. Thus, guiding supplies the most essential need of education—the development of character, which is the most neglected thing in our country. The present system of girls' education has created a big gap and a cleavage between home and school life. Our girls, with all their degrees and experiences of school life, are unfit to help in domestic matters.

Guiding, with its subjects, such as homemaking, mothercraft, sick-nursing, child welfare, and social service, serves the greatest purpose of education and bridges the gulf. Homemaking is an essential subject in a girl's life in a country where 98 per cent of the girls are destined to marry, and where the homes of the majority of the people are not well-organized. The Guides, with their skilled knowledge of that art introduce a new spirit in all that pertains to home management and make the homes healthy, happy and attractive. In these days of high prices and shortage of domestic help, the knowledge of homemaking gives them power and creates a delightful feeling of self-reliance and independence.

It is needless to say how the child marriage system of our country has been the chief cause of the infant and girl-mothers' mortality and morbidity. Inexperienced girls in their early teens are married and are supposed to face the great responsibility of motherhood. So much of the health of a child depends upon the mother's efficient care and upon her creating healthy and regular habits in it. Mothercraft requires a good deal of practical experience which is provided in a well-organized Guides company. They are taught to handle dolls and how to bathe, feed, and nurse them when a supposed sickness comes. Thus,

Guiding prepares girls to face the great responsibility of motherhood. In this country, when illness or ill health comes to a household, it is usually due to improper feeding, insufficient fresh air, and want of exercise. Guides, with their authentic knowledge of sick nursing, are a source of help in emergencies and are competent and intelligent nurses.

No one can deny the fact that Indians, and especially ladies, are amazingly impractical and consequently inefficient. They lack initiative and driving power. The educational system of our country, being theoretical, has made the girls both psychologically and physiologically disinclined to work. The idea has gained ground in them that manual labour, and even domestic work, is below their dignity. Guiding has a practical bias, and it is the practical side of education. It develops the spirit of adventure in them and gives a new zest for life. It develops a taste for hobbies and handicraft by providing vocational or industrial training. A liking for handwork might ultimately give a girl a living opening for her life's work, when the struggle for existence among the poor is growing keener and keener. Vocational training removes, from their minds, wrong notions about manual labour.

Physical health and a healthy condition of mind are the basis upon which all mental education must necessarily be founded. Not only is the physically unfit girl likely to be below the average of mental capacity, but the actual development of the brain is largely influenced by means of physical activities. Guiding aims at the improvement of the general physique, prevention and correction of faulty movement, and the teaching of a good posture for the body. It includes games, athletic sports, swimming, riding, and dancing. Such activities form good habits. The physical stamina among the school-going girls of our country is at its lowest ebb; hence, the value of Girl Guiding, in the education of girls, is indispensable.

The Guides' training is designed to fill the leisure time of girls. The long vacations are days of wasting on the plea of well-earned rest. Adolescence is an age when girls like to do something or other and they cannot be kept quiet. If their energy is not directed towards useful activities, they fall an easy prey to harmful ones. The Guides' training gives them helpful and useful activities and encourages them to learn plenty of things by using their hands, eyes, ears, and voices. It helps them to do good turns and directs their minds towards useful activities. Vocational training satisfies their creative instincts and develops the spirit of self-dependence in them. It saves them from unsuitable companionship and its harmful influences.

In school, one is apt to develop the spirit of competition by offering rewards and punishment, praise and blame, and other varied appeals to the pupils as an incentive to effort. But the relationships established by such temptations are neither lasting nor healthy. On the other hand, they develop the spirit of rivalry. Guiding, unlike this, develops team spirit and unity. The members steadily keep the welfare and dignity of the whole company in view. Guiding develops collective interest and individual efficiency. If the aim of Guiding is the same as that of education, and if it supplements and complements education, how should it be run? Will school mistresses, with their theoretical education and with a little smattering knowledge of Guiding, be efficient Guides? Will they inspire Guides' ideals in the hopeful? The answer is an emphatic 'no'. Guiding needs quite a different treatment; it needs the service of selfless workers. Those who work not for remuneration or fame, but for the love of the work and for the sake of the work, should be interested in the Guides movement. It needs the lead of women of broad outlook, keen insight, and courageous vision. The inspiration from such leaders should give a new life and new orientation, altogether, to the movement. They should be able to make people realize the usefulness of the movement.

The Guides' organization, to be progressive, should be supported by the people themselves with endowments, subscriptions, donations, or other help. It should be self-supporting and should be an independent organization. It must be free from the control of the education department and there must be a systematic blending and harmonious cooperation between the two organizations—the education department and the Guides' movement. There should be mutual understanding and help between the three fundamental educative factors—the home, the school, and Guiding.

The Guides' Movement should be made more popular among the people if it is to make a wide appeal to them. The present world is called the world of reasoning, and people being sensible cannot be taken in by mere profession or by demonstrations like rallies. Success in anything does not come by talk; one has to achieve it. The deeds of Guides, either in the service of home or of society, must speak.

The method of training of Guides in our country is very unsatisfactory. In a state where there are eight big districts there should be at least one training centre in each one of them. One permanent training centre in the headquarters for higher training, like an ordinary diploma and the chief's diploma, is necessary. Each training centre should be under the direction of a commandant and it should be open for certain periods in the year, where definite instruction in elementary and advanced Guides' work should be given. Lectures and practical demonstrations should be arranged often. Guiding should be made compulsory in all schools, colleges, boardings, and hostels by the department of education, but the responsibility of running companies should be entrusted to the Guides organization.

In this country, every kind of activity is given too much vetting by the government. This has made people indifferent to their own duties of social service, and to look to government aid for every thing. This mentality of dependence on the government support has made them think that nothing can be done without government patronage. This attitude of the people can be compared to a certain extent to that of parasites. It has killed the spirit of individuality and initiative in them. No society and no organization can prosper so long as it depends upon the support of others. The Guides' movement needs the help of a selfless leader to reorganize, to inspire, and to encourage the women of the country to take to Guiding, and to do their duty to the progress and uplift of the young generation of their country.

31

The Girl Guides Movement in India

As presented by Mrs Hussain at the Council Fire Meeting of the eighth World Conference of the International Girl Guides and Girl Scouts held at Adelboden, Switzerland, October 1934

In presenting a report for India it is necessary to bring forward some of the many problems which we have to face and to overcome. India is spoken of as a country but, in reality, it is more like a continent, containing many countries, differing largely in race, language, creed, and custom. The population of India is 370 million of which only about 15 per cent can read and write.

To give some idea of distances, let me say that, if Miss Mallinson and I, the delegates from India, wished to call on each other there, we should have to travel day and night for a week. These difficulties are, however, overcome in Guiding as is shown by the fact that each year, when the All-India camp is held, Guiders travel thousands of miles. Last November, the camp was held at Lahore, and Her Excellency the Vicereine flew from Delhi to spend a day at this camp. She took part in the World Flag Ceremony, to which fourteen provinces brought world flags with their provincial badges embroidered on them. Her Excellency also encourages prominent Indians to take an interest in the movement by becoming vice-patrons.

At this camp were Guiders of all creeds, Brahmins, other Hindus, Muhammadans, Parsees, Sikhs, Jews, Roman Catholics, and Protestants. The wonder is that all these types sleep and eat and work together. And, still more wonderful is the way in which each Guide plays her part in working for the success of the whole. For instance, Her Highness the Maharani of Sangli, when asked to take the salute at morning colours, excused herself on the grounds of being otherwise occupied with her washing up patrol. Her Highness the Maharani of Mysore has shown her appreciation of the movement by giving a large donation and His Highness presented the Guides with a beautiful headquarters building. The foundation of this building was laid by the chief guide of Mysore, her Highness the Yuvarani. On this occasion, the Guides presented His Highness with a piece of embroidery, the trefoil in gold on a red ground the colour of the state flag. This was much appreciated by His Highness, both for the work itself and for the sentiment behind it. Messages were also received from the Yuvraj,[*] who is the chief scout of Mysore, and from the world chief scout and the world chief guide themselves.

In Kashmir, too, the Maharani has shown keen interest in the Guides of her state. Last autumn, all the Guides and Bluebirds were invited to tea at the palace. Her Highness

---

[*] Now HH the Maharaja of Mysore.

was much entertained by the programme, which was 'A day in Camp in Miniature'. Tiny tents were pitched, the Guides went to sleep in them, woke up, made tea, did a few exercises, staged a fracture which had to be dealt with during the meal, washed a baby, and ended up with a campfire. The young prince, who was then two and a half years old, made delightful remarks, such as: 'Funny girls!' 'Broken Leg!'. He, himself, gave each Guide and Bluebird a present as they left, looking up at each one with a most seraphic smile.

Her Highness the Maharani of Travancore translated *Girl Guiding* into the language of her own people. The Promise and Laws are the same as in Great Britain. But, for the second class, the Child Nurse Test is taken instead of Morse. This is most important, as the legal marriage age is still only fourteen and infant mortality terribly high. The fact that girls who become Guides are taught to look after a child appeals very much to the mothers. Gentleness, patience, and forbearance are striking characteristics of Indian womanhood.

The following extract from the *Report of Guiding in India* will show better than I can what is being achieved:

> Only one and a half hours a week, and yet Bluebirds' training does leave its mark on the small girl and bring into her life many lovely things that are sadly lacking, at any rate in the case of many Indian children. To be free for one and a half hours to learn things for yourself without the baby who is forever clinging to your hip, to learn to see the beauty in

the sunset and the palms, to hear stories of adventure and romance, to dance and sing and make believe; should not such things be the heritage of every child? Yet to how many of India's little toiling daughters are they denied?

At first, it was among the more fortunate children who had the privilege of going to schools that Bluebird flocks made their appearance. Now the movement is spreading to out-of-the-way villages and to the children of illiterate folk.

In Bengal, coolie communities are being reached, as in Rajshahi where the flock caters for little Muhammadan girls who have never been to school. In Cawnpore, it is hoped to start a flock among the mill children. Bombay reports one flock working among children of the depressed classes and another in a blind school. Hyderabad State reports a flock in the Brahmin community.

In a country where Guiding is frequently looked upon with suspicion, the Bluebird flock can pave the way for the training of older girls. This is what seems to be happening in many districts. Sixteen new flocks are reported from the Punjab this year, nearly all in areas untouched before. Bluebird work is only the beginning, and we hope many of the children will pass on to be Guides. But, in India, due to early marriage and other connected customs, all will never have that privilege; so, while we can, let us train the Indian child (who will so soon have the responsibility of wifehood and motherhood thrust upon her) in character and intelligence, skill and handicraft, physical health and development, and service to others.

As for the Rangers, during last year the Rangers proved themselves good citizens in:

(a) Helping regularly with Guides, Bluebirds, or Wolfcubs in schools for blind, deaf, or otherwise defective children and in a reformatory for boys;

(b) Visiting regularly and teaching games, handicrafts, etc. in a children's remand home, and helping in a nursery school in a mill area;

(c) Collecting and repairing old toys, for the Red Cross Society;

(d) Teaching and demonstrating village hygiene and sanitation and helping with adult education in villages.

A large number of the Rangers are Cadet Rangers, learning the joys and responsibilities of Guiding with the definite purpose of future service in the Guide Movement. Companies of Cadet Rangers are to be found now in the majority of teachers' training colleges and schools and even in arts and medical colleges, and from them will come both future Guiders and women prepared to take an intelligent and active interest in the Guide Movement. Some of the Cadet Rangers are already translating songs, games, and general Guide literature into various vernaculars, and helping in other ways to adapt Guiding to Indian conditions.

Every year Guides—British, Indian, and Anglo-Indian—are trained at the YMCA Training Centre, Ootacamund. Other training is held in different parts of India three times a year. India will always be proud of Miss Rustomjee, a Parsee, who took her Red Cord Diploma with such flying colours.

The total number of Guides in India is now 29,741, an increase of 6,262 since 1932. These numbers include one blind company, two leper companies, one leper flock, one company in a rescue home, one company in a borstal jail, and lone Guides.

32

Heredity

A contribution to a discussion held in Bangalore under the auspices of the Bangalore Discussion Group

❝The Cornerstone of Mendelism, Lamarckism, and Darwinism deservedly hold the honour of having made the world think in terms of evolution ...' These men not only proved their theories through facts and experiments but also by their powerful explanations which influenced the thoughts of the world for one or two generations, even after their deaths. They put forward and emphasized one or two essential factors to the exclusion of others. This gave rise to controversy, but none of the theorists have arrived at a very satisfactory answer to our queries.

Mendel's theory of the cornerstone applies only when the parents have contrasted characteristics which do not blend. The result is the dominant character showing itself in the proportion of three to one over the recessive. By further experiment, he proved that the ratio sometimes varies, he emphasized that the physical and mental aptitude or capacity, or lack of it, is settled to some extent by its heredity. His theory is based on the proposition that no two persons are alike.

Lamarck stressed the part played by the living organism and offered a natural explanation of evolution: that creatures have an inward urge to realize their needs, such as intellectual, physical, social, and moral, to adapt themselves to their environment, change their natural habits, and even modify their bodily structure. His latter assumption has given rise to a great controversy which has not been finally settled.

What are the essentials of Darwin's doctrine? He laid stress on the following: that living creatures are very prolific and so they have to struggle for food; that variations occur and are transmissible; and that the result is the survival of the fittest and the elimination of the unfit. He recognized two kinds of innate variations and ignored their origins.

The theory of transmission is accepted by other theorists. McDougal says that the modifications acquired by the parents are found in the offspring. He adds that the process of transmission is very slow and gradual. The children easily learn what is useful from their parents. Mr Bernard Shaw says that different species of animals have sprung up from a common ancestry, and that higher forms of life have evolved from lower forms by a process of gradual and orderly change.

Let us examine the opposite view of the theory of transmission. Galton says that the body grows by the multiplication of cells from the germ cell. These productive cells take no part in the development of the body and are continuous from one generation to another. 'Thus, the parent is rather the trustee of the germ plasm than the producer of the child'. Professor Hugo De Vries of Amsterdam and Sir John Adams refuted the theory of transmission and said that the appearance of the parents special characteristics in their children may not be due to heredity but to having been brought up in the company of their parents. They introduced a new term called 'social heredity'.

What is the word 'heredity' itself? Ross says it is a word used to cover a number of familiar facts which may be summed up in propositions such as 'like tends to beget like' and 'a chip of the old block'. These are often used in daily talk when one means that children receive mental and physical traits from their parents. McBride opined that the word 'heredity' itself is a misleading metaphor drawn from human laws of succession in property. People attribute much to heredity, that is, rather due to environment.

Mere learned words are often a means of concealing ignorance of facts. A plain man believes implicitly in any idea put forward before him. No one can dare deny the fact that children are born with a certain inborn aptitude which develops with the help of external forces. The present world is rightly called the 'age of reasoning'. No one believes in things implicitly without discussing both sides of a question. In these days, one finds that people are mostly after artificial things, so artificial selection has replaced the natural one. The idea of keeping up the mental or physical fitness of the race is no longer held now. Medical research, with its discoveries, has improved the methods of living a healthy life, and specific guidance about the care of babies and mothers has proved that the unfit are not eliminated. The improved scientific methods of production have helped people to produce enough for living beings. Different acts passed now and then to mitigate suffering have helped people to live longer. The development of education provides equal opportunity to all, irrespective of caste and race, to get intellectual, physical, or vocational education according to the inborn aptitude of the individual. The old theory that only a few gifted people deserve education has disappeared from the world. Hence, we see that common sense and the fruit of experience should not be surrendered to any theory, however plausible it may be. Although heredity plays a part, yet it is not the prime factor in human life.

33

Woman as an Individual

Investigations made by the psychologists of today have revealed the fact that there is absolutely no particular intellectual difference between men and women. Both of them are born with an equipment of inborn tendencies and capacities which induce certain responses to certain stimuli. These tendencies are highly modifiable and they are conditioned by environmental contact. The instincts, emotions, and feelings of both man and woman have the same effect and influence on body and mind. The personalities of both develop on the same principles and are cramped under the same circumstances.

A woman, as an individual, possesses a definite view of her destiny as a unit of life. The nature of the universe is such that it provides opportunities for everyone to maintain, in some way or other, the kind of individuality necessary for the final working out of human action. Individuality of action and thought are the highest aspirations of the human mind. The highest delight of the individual lies in her gradual growth, in self-possession, in uniqueness, and in her intensity of activity as a person. Her individuality develops with the free play of her desires and other human instincts. In consequence of her developed individuality, it makes it impossible for her to bear the burden of another and do what is not to her own personal satisfaction. Whatever maybe her final fate, it does not mean the loss of her own individuality but it maybe she is suppressed or cramped under unfavourable and trying circumstances. The control of her individual activity shows that she is causally free and uses her own free will. The Holy Quran emphatically says that 'man is the trustee of a free personality which he accepted at his peril' and rejects the idea of redemption.

The word 'I' has its own significance. It is simply an indivisible object. A human being is a gregarious animal. She may be one of the group, yet she is different from it. Her membership of the group makes her a specific being in her own eyes. The idea of self and self-respect is foremost in human beings. Individuality of a person does much to give her a clear idea of herself and her powers. Her cooperation with others only creates a new world, and ideas, in her which she exclusively uses to her own interest. Individuality of a person is conducive to that person's progress. It raises a person above dependence and develops the habit of self-control and self-reliance. It directs her intellectual power to discover what is the most right thing for her to do and what is the most worth doing. New efforts are made, and new ideas are collected by her, which increase the value of the self. The self, in the act of persevering, judging, and acting, is appreciated and its prominence is kept steadily in view. The idea of self-regard and self-prominence in an environment of contradiction and repression is subordinated.

Human consciousness forms the centre of human thought and action. It is a living element in a human being and it is the point upon which one's own personality is built on. It is a disciplining factor and helps realization of self and the permanence of self-respect. Realization of self is possible only when there is freedom of thought and action, and freedom from contradiction. Human consciousness, in its matured form, points to the highest level of personality which is attributed as a characteristic of an individual. But, in actual life, especially in the life of a woman, it is taken for a passive element and as a passive state of expectation. There can be no error as pressing and grave as this. It is a state in which the individual catches an idea of fresh aspects of self-realization and prepares herself for adjustment to those aspects. Elimination of unfavourable ones follows suit. Thus, a person tries to possess a clear and mature consciousness which results in the development of inner experiences and that of decision and judgement.

A desire for a certain object is natural in human beings. It is essentially one's own. When the purpose is personal, it becomes stronger. One leaves no stone unturned to achieve the end. The satisfaction of a desire means one's own enjoyment, and its denial results in dissatisfaction and ill feeling. The satisfaction of another's desire does not mean her own. A person may sympathise with somebody's suffering but she cannot experience the extent of another's pain. One's pleasure and pain are one's own and they form a part and parcel of one's own being. Similarly, feelings, hates, loves, judgements, and resolutions are exclusively one's own.

The development of these instincts depends upon one's own environmental contact. They need free play and interaction for their development. The dissatisfaction of one's desire does not mean its destruction but only its suppression. It may be aggressive at any time as opportunity occurs.

An action is nothing but a desire put into practise. 'Practise makes perfect'. One's action develops one's experience. It is only the result of a series of acts. Actions and experience mutually refer to one another and hold together by the unity of directive purpose. One's success in one's purpose leads to another of the higher kind. Success in attempts develops one's attitude for activities and aspirations. The action and experience of an individual, though mutually independent, are yet united. The changes in both run exactly on parallel lines with a pre-established harmony. The power to act freely is a constant factor in the life of an individual, and it prepares an individual for a future career. In surroundings where an independent action is not possible, the experience remains inefficient. The individuality is killed by disuse and, without, it there is no free thinking and acting. Thought dissects and analyses one's feelings, which help the formation of a strong willpower. Individuality is the root of everything good and decent. The progress of humanity, with its cultures and civilizations, is only possible when the individuality of the human being is maintained and developed.

In a polygamous marriage, a woman is called upon to live in an environment which invades her private life. She is compelled to subordinate all her instincts and emotions to the repressive environment. Her natural life cannot be maintained and she begins to live a dual life by reducing it to a mere mechanical system. Her thoughts are only concentrated only on making her life in the house possible. The sense of dependence on others, for her happiness, effects a great change in her character. Implicit obedience to whimsical and fanciful mankind has made her cease to think in terms of her own individuality. The general tendency among men, to think of her as an inefficient and reasonless being, has made her ideas limited and has narrowed her vision and outlook on life. Living constantly in an atmosphere of ignorance and restriction, her power of striving is killed. Her sense of reliance is a thing of the past, the sense of responsibility is almost destroyed with disuse, and her dynamic power of command is lost. She resigns herself, as a mere puppet, to the standards of the man-made world and to those made by her rival. Being an experienced hand, the latter possesses a commanding influence on developed and fixed modes. As there is no bond of sympathy between these women, their inclinations and aims are of opposite types. Often, a spirit of jealousy, dissatisfaction, and ill feeling is exhibited in their thoughts and deeds.

The principle on which individuality is developed is respect for the person and a considerate and living treatment of her feelings and pains. Liberty to do what she thinks dignified and decent, and a mere suggestion as to the harmful consequences of her actions if she does wrong, are needed. It is a serious error to think that a woman who is carefully guarded at all times, and checked at every action and thought, can lead a successful life and manage her own affairs. Efficiency does not come by mere talk. A person should have a grounding in self-action. Personality does not come to one as a right. It is to be achieved through personal effort and freedom. A strong-willed husband maintains a weak-willed wife. A strong-willed rival, in cooperation with the weak-willed man, produces a human figure (her home rival) with the characteristics of a lamb—a woman with a negative character.

34

Potentialities of the Future

I have, so far, attempted to take stock of the religious theory which sanctions women equal rights and status as man and which makes no difference between man and woman in secular and spiritual matters or of the treatment meted out to her in daily life. I have also dealt, in detail, with the causes that are responsible for the divergence between theory and practise. What are they? The neglect of her intellectual, social, physical, economic, and moral conditions, the lack of opportunities for their development, the system of polygamy and that of the hoarding of numerous women in the zenana on the pretext of protecting them from evils, the authoritative attitude of man towards her, her very life of inactivity where there are little chances of using her tendencies, talents, and capacities, and all these factors have been the chief cause of the degenerations of the Indian nation in general and that of Muslims in particular. But what about the years to come? Can her condition in our country be expected to solve the difficulties, breakdown the barriers, and bridge the gulf between theory and practise by creating a new era of comradeship, an ideal companionship, and an equal cooperation between men and women in all the affairs of life? Can it be so improved as to make her an asset, a real help, a source from which all that is good and noble for the progress of a nation may be drawn, and make her stand on her own feet and be an equal among equals? This quotation speaks volumes for the fact.

Who shall raise and redeem the nation? Who if not you, you who are the educators and preceptors of it—will make it stand on its feet, stand erect among the nations an equal among equals, efficient to work out its own evolution and fulfil its God-given mission in the life of humanity.

What potentialities are there for the future?

The world is rapidly changing and is becoming one neighbourhood. Old barriers of time and space are broken down. Environment is constantly changing and giving birth to new ideas, ideals, and fashions. The environmental contact is so great that it makes people change their tendencies and to adjust themselves to it. The change, in some cases, is a real one and in others imitative; yet there is change. Association between nation and nation is growing so close that international problems of a varying nature are arising. Some of them cause friction, no doubt, but some unite the nations to exchange their ideas and ideals. Consequently, the people of our country have begun to think of preserving their own culture, traditions, and civilization and to take pride in them. The contributions made by different nations for human welfare are appreciated, and attempts have been made to understand the customs, ideals, and cultures of others with a view to seeking a common interest in them. Great modern thinkers of our country have been making a real contribution to the welfare and progress of their communities in particular, and of Indians in general. These have been the real incentives in developing a spirit of self-realization, self-responsibility, and self-respect in most of them. A demand for self-expression, political liberty, religious freedom, social equality, and economic justice is expressed everywhere. A growing desire to serve one's own country faithfully is felt in the united lives of men, women, and youth. There is unanimous support for women's education and progress. Equal rights and suffrage have been granted to them by many of the governments all over India through the passing of the following resolution. 'That sex shall form no disqualification to women entering any position or profession for which she shows herself capable.' The motto of the most advanced countries: 'Educate that you may be free' is followed here by the majority of men.

The spirit of the times is permeating the hemisphere of womanhood with the necessity for progress. The sense of self-depreciation, shyness, and of inferiority complex found among them formerly is disappearing gradually. The wide current of progressive ideas sweeping all over the world has reached even the more secluded corners of the Muslim women's world. Women in general, on their own initiative and through their own growing surge of desire for self-expression, have broken down the old barriers of custom, caste, creed, and seclusion. Their efforts are amalgamated with those of men in the progress and regeneration of their nation. There is a new team spirit to be found in them. A feeling of freedom and of equality is expressed in different ways. The wearing of jewels and expensive clothes is taken as a symbol of submissiveness to man. The ideal life, 'simple living and high thinking', is followed by many, especially those who are educated. The fight for equal rights, status, and a democratic form of social organization is not an uncommon thing nowadays. Indian women today want to be self-reliant, self-respecting, and responsible.

As a result of this attitude and spirit, and by their insistent efforts, they have won a special place in the home, in society, and in the governments of their country. Many of them have become the leaders, public speakers, philanthropic workers, presidents of ladies' conferences, organizers, and secretaries of different associations. They are the active members of representative and legislative assemblies of their countries, world conferences and national congresses are attended by them. The granting of equal suffrage and rights has been a driving force in them in securing greater educational facilities for girls. The advance in education for women has been extended so much lately that women's universities and colleges have sprung up almost overnight and are overcrowded with them.

The child, as a prospective member of the future generation and of the nation, is receiving increasing recognition. The study of his instincts, capacities, interests, and his gradual development is emphasized at home, in school, and in society. He is taken as the centre of the educational process. The intellectual, social, physical, moral, and religious aspects are taken into consideration and developed systematically. His experiences are drawn from suitable books, observation, inquiry, and experimentation. The development of his mind, character, and personality are taken as the fundamental principles of his education. The practical side of education is not neglected. He is made to learn by doing. His creative activities are provided with necessary facilities to make his school life interesting.

Praise and encouragement should be given to all the pioneer workers of our country. In the field of progress, their work is indispensable. Their objective is a high one. They should not be discouraged with obstacles. The more difficulties there are, the more courage they need to face them and the more power they need to surmount them. There is no progress without effort. This is necessary, not only from the workers but also by others. The more effective it is, the greater joy it gives and the greater is the satisfaction it leaves behind. The only thing that is necessary is a strong confidence and faith in one's own efforts.

Appendix

'Women's Rights and Duties as a Citizen'

[In addition to the speech on 'East-West in Cooperation,' Iqbalunnisa also presented a talk at another panel at the twelfth conference of International Alliance of Women for Suffrage and Equal Citizenship (IAWSEC) in Istanbul, Turkey from 18–25 April 1935 titled 'Women's Rights and Duties as a Citizen'. The speech, not included in the original text of *Changing India*, is reproduced below.[1] In the speech, Iqbalunnisa discusses responsibilities and duties involved in motherhood and presents a gendered notion of citizenship. The speech illustrates the importance of familial relations to the articulation of political concepts.]

Dr Asiya Alam

I feel quite nervous to deal with the subject, especially in a country which is not only advanced but very well advanced in different lines and in different aspects of life such as socially, morally, spiritually, and intellectually. The developed personality of the women and their social and helpful nature seems almost an unborn attitude of their character. The grandeur of the monuments and their national architecture, the coins, the generous hospitality and everything of this place has made me feel entirely in a new world. Especially so, when I compare the Muslims of other parts with all of you. I honestly tell you that

---

1. Iqbalunnisa Hussain, 'Women's Rights and Duties as a Citizen' IAW papers, 1935, Box 3, Sophia Smith Collection.

not only the Muslim women of the other parts of the world and not only the women of the world, but also the whole humanity at large have to be proud of you. The equal and just treatment of womanhood of this country can easily be taken as a model of future civilization by many countries, if not by the whole world. For the success of the present conditions not only the women have to be most heartily congratulated but also the just, brave, and noble men of the place. No words are too strong to describe appropriately the success of your achievement and my talk to you is like an old saying or in other words it is like a tiny dot on the edge of a big surface.

Coming to the proper subject of my talk, woman as an obedient and accomplished wife. Education is an instrument of spiritual, moral, intellectual, and social decoration. It develops one's personality, character and it brings up a woman for her own sake and for the sake of her country and the nation. How obviously fallacious the argument is to say that an educated woman is a disobedient wife! On the other hand the more educated the woman is the more she understands herself and the more she realizes her rights and duties to her husband, children, society, and the nation at large. The more educated she is, the better considerate she feels. It is not too strong to say that she is a blessing in disguise to one and all. By education I do not mean the primary education, which has been made compulsory by many countries. The officials take great pride in it and very proudly profess that their country has compulsory education. 'A little knowledge is a dangerous thing' and a woman with that smattering knowledge is dangerous too.

Wife is an intellectual companion, physical companionship of a woman is not everything and it is equivalent to animal life. Human beings have greater needs and they are superior and supreme to animal life such as the moral, social, spiritual, and intellectual needs. These needs are satisfied by each other in the way of living together. Once a very rich man married a poor and ugly but a learned woman. They lived a happy life. One day the wife composed a few lines. The gist of it was a question put to her husband asking what made him marry her. He replies that he had certain needs and they had to be satisfied by a second person and he found in her the fittest person to satisfy his necessities. Hence he married her irrespective of her beauty and wealth. If man's harshness and roughness of nature is left to himself it develops into cruel barbarity, making him unfit for domestic life. The woman repairs these natural defects with her tact, culture, and gentleness of manner and love.

Mother, the best and the first educator of her children. As we know education begins from the cradle and mother bring the privileged person to be nearer the child at this tender age has a splendid opportunity to lay the foundation of education. The real meaning of education is not passing of exams and acquiring diploma. But it is a capacity and tendency to adjust oneself to the circumstances and to respond to the changing environmental stimuli. It is a power within that makes one to face the difficulties boldly and efficiently. Every child in the world comes with a certain inborn capacity and tendency, which calls for the certain response to certain stimuli. It is developed gradually and methodically by the mother by supplying the stimulus. The mental faculties such as observation, imagination, thinking, expression, etc. develop from the very young age, from the age of two or three. At the age of five or six a child feels an impelling force within to express himself or herself in different ways. It may be by replying or writing, drawing, painting, music, and even dancing. Expression causes happiness and satisfaction to the child and if it is denied he feels miserable and dissatisfied.

This is supposed be the greatest power for one's development and progress. It is very keen in young children and is not altogether absent in elderly people. The frequent speeches and lectures are the result of this force within that make people accept the offers and to get themselves satisfied by conveying their ideas to others.

A sensible mother encourages the child to express in different ways as there is no 'impression without expression'. On the other hand an illiterate mother being herself as innocent in intellect as the child not only suppresses these faculties but kills them. No wonder that 60 to 70 per cent of the people feel nervous to express themselves in more than two sentences. If the ignorance is added to the so-called blessing of numberless children, the development of intellect is made secondary, if not ignored and building up of the body at the expense of brain is kept in the foremost by the illiterate mother.

Mother, the moulder of moral character is as important a person as the educator. The process of character development is a slow and a gradual growth. It needs constant watch. It is the result of personal contact with life. It is not an imposed object but an acquired and achieved ideal. Character comes even before the intellect begins so it is the primary duty of the mother to develop this, the most important aspect of human life.

Woman is the maker of a happy home. She is naturally disposed to take interest in it. Her decoration and efficient management, if added to her gentleness of manner and persuasive power is enough to supply the needs of a happy home.

There is nothing more interesting to an unmarried woman or to a widow or to a married woman who has no care of her children than the social and public service. It is her first and the foremost duty to enlighten the society. She is sure to find an eternal joy and everlasting happiness in every success of her efforts as a politician or as an educator or a social worker.

A nature to be brave and noble ought to be taught through its women first. The destiny of a nation lies to a greater extent in the hands of the women. They are the educator and the circulator of the humanity at large. The nation's excellence depends upon the culture and discrimination of its womanhood.

Woman as a teacher is emphasized by the modern educational thinkers and the psychologists that every Jack and Dick cannot be a born teacher. A born teacher is one, who is an embodiment of love, impartiality, gentleness of manner, and persuasive power, and she takes delight in succouring misery. She has a lot of girl spirit in her and feels herself as one of the members she teaches. She is an elderly sister to her pupils but not an autocratic ruler with unlimited powers. She does not take the child's mind as an empty vessel to pour out a lot of rubbish that she gathered for years. She should take it as a tender plant that needs gentle treatment and loving and sympathetic behaviour, as it is expressed in the following quotation:

The teacher is simply to live the life and the student is to develop her nature under the magnetic influence of her personality. It is heart speaking to heart, character moulding character, the awakened soul of the teacher rousing the dormant soul of the taught. The silent influence exercised by the teacher awakens in the disciple, a sense of power and strength. It is life kindling life, thought influencing thought.

Iqbalunnisa Hussain

2 April 1935

Index